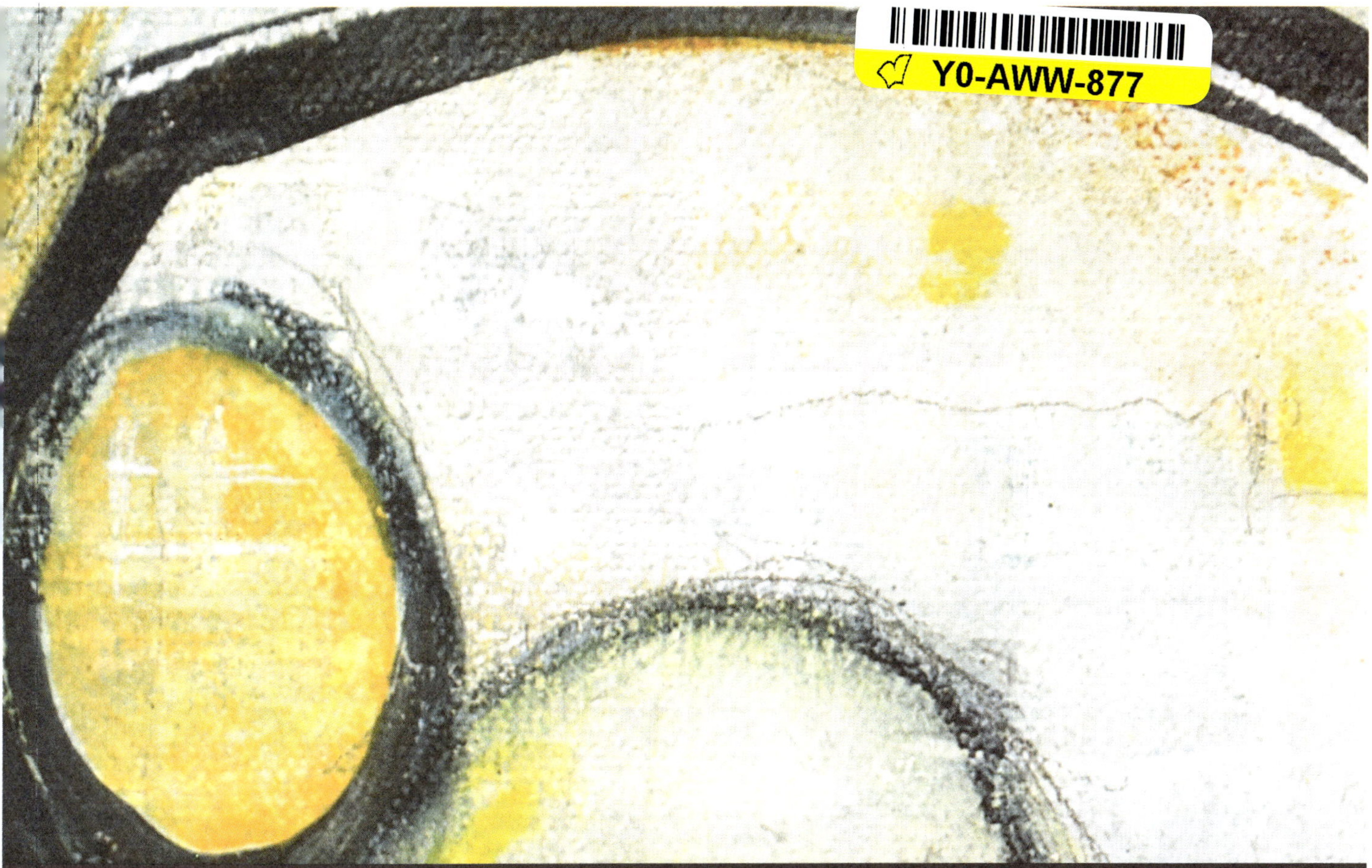

STA 296

STATISTICAL METHODS & MOTIVATIONS SUPPLEMENT FOR ALL SECTIONS

William Rayens

VAN-GRINER LEARNING

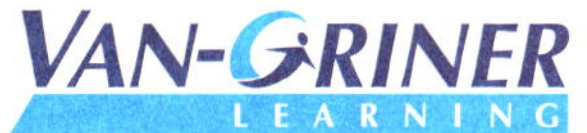

Statistical Methods & Motivations

STA 296
Supplement for All Sections

About the Cover Design: The artwork on the cover was done by Jamie Van Landuyt, a studio artist working in Cincinnati. Just as her abstract art involves layering and obscured compositional elements, so do statistics as numbers belie the underlying conceptual complexity.

Printed in the United States of America
10 9 8 7 6 5 4 3 2 1
ISBN: 978-1-64565-096-6

Van-Griner Publishing
Cincinnati, Ohio
www.van-griner.com

President: Dreis Van Landuyt
Project Manager: Brenda Schwieterman
Customer Care Lead: Lauren Wendel

Rayens 65-096-6 Su21
322621

From the Author

This workbook has been created especially for your course and is a subset of the larger book *Beyond the Numbers: Student-Centered Activities for Learning Statistical Reasoning* 7th edition by Dr. William Rayens. All data sets are available online at www.statconcepts.com or from your instructor. Best wishes for an outstanding semester!

Table of Contents

Introduction

Beyond the Numbers

Student-Centered Activities for Learning Statistical Reasoning

Overview of the Workbook

Dr. William Rayens has taught statistical reasoning at the University of Kentucky (U.K.) for about thirty-five years. This book addresses the needs of the statistical reasoning community, as well as the ever-growing universal need for statistically-literate citizens. There are several conceptually-focused statistical reasoning books on the market, but *Beyond the Numbers: A Student-Centered Approach to Learning Statistical Reasoning* is distinct in two noteworthy ways:

1. **This text is unambiguously focused on statistical reasoning.** Our goal is to help students competently consume statistical ideas that meet them where they live—both academically and personally. If you measure worth by the number of computations performed within this text, then it might seem light. If you measure worth based on the weight of the statistical reasoning that the chosen methods surface, then the book is heavy, indeed. Computations and exposure to different methods are still valued since they surely increase students' life skills. But we have been careful not to allow students to be distracted by unnecessary computations since it has been our experience that they often find those easier to grasp than the more important understanding of what is gained from such computations.

2. **This text is designed to shift the primary responsibility of learning to the student.** Borrowing the words of STEM (science, technology, engineering, and mathematics) educator Robert Talbert, the goal of this shift is to change the mindset of the student from a "renter" to an "owner." In a classroom of renters, fees are paid and the management is expected to deliver. In a classroom of owners, however, students realize that it is their responsibility to engage, absorb, and retain. The instructor's difficult, but important, job is to prepare an environment in which that can happen. This book, mostly through how its exercises are structured, is designed to help facilitate students' transition from renters to owners. While the content is carefully constructed to prepare students to do the accompanying exercises, they will be asked repeatedly to read, comprehend, and assimilate in order to complete them.

Relevancy

If you are going to ask students to be actively involved in their own learning, it is important you *engage* them. With examples that are relevant to their day-to-day encounters, students are more likely to relate to the material. Once the connection is made, students tend to be drawn into the content and consequently become more involved in their own learning. To help make these critical connections, we have been careful in our choice of exercises. Throughout the book we address current topics that are not only illustrative in content, but are also relatable to the student. Some examples include the following:

- A February 2014 study on gay marriage to facilitate the construction and interpretation of a confidence interval, when the margin of error is given.
- A 2014 Gallup Organization–Purdue University report on the effects of one's college choice to introduce the idea of using confidence intervals to make hypothesis-testing like decisions.
- A study on the efficacy of social networking systems as instructional tools to demonstrate the empirical rule.

Another key to engagement is the presentation of the material. We have deliberately chosen a chapter design that is more open, friendly, and less formal than other textbooks that cover similar material. Don't be fooled; the material is there. We have opted for a format that is more student-appealing.

Software as Part of a College Education

All students, from liberal arts majors to engineers, need to know how to use basic software suites to manipulate numbers, perform calculations, and create graphs. Sobered by how few students learned these basic skills as they progressed through college, we have long endeavored to integrate them naturally into the material in this book. While we encourage our students to use any software, even online applets, we illustrate some graphical and summary computation throughout with Microsoft Excel. The specific software doesn't really matter, but students should probably have some basic exposure before graduating.

About the Author

Dr. William Rayens is Professor and the Dr. Bing Zhang Endowed Department Chair in the Dr. Bing Zhang Department of Statistics at the University of Kentucky. Rayens has an extensive research record focused primarily on the development of multivariate and multi-way statistical methodologies mostly related to problems in chemistry and the neurosciences. He has mentored several Ph.D. students and has been honored at both the College and the University level as an outstanding teacher. Rayens also served as Assistant Provost for General Education during which time he was tasked with implementing new general education reforms at the University of Kentucky, the first changes to that program in almost 30 years. Rayens created STA 210: Introduction to Statistical Reasoning in 2010, and designed the one-of-a-kind Technologically Enhanced Active Learning rooms in the Jacobs Science Building where he and his instructors are genuinely privileged to teach STA 210 and use this book.

THEME 1

Sampling

BEYOND THE NUMBERS 1.1

Prudent Survey Design

Name: ____ Section Number: ________

To be graded, all assignments must be completed and submitted on the original book page.

EXHIBIT 1

Monkey Tutoring

SurveyMonkey®, a free online survey tool, has constructed a simple survey to help us understand that long before we can discuss statistical science and surveys, we must be comfortable with some basic rules of survey design. Read each question, and in the space to the right of the question, indicate what is wrong with the question (if anything).

Questions	Your Comments
1. How many times have you used Adobe Acrobat during the last calendar year? ________________________________	
2. When typing a letter, I typically use: ☐ Word ☐ Adobe Acrobat ☐ Photoshop ☐ A word processor	
3. The Mac operating system rarely gets infected by viruses, and therefore, the Department of Education should only purchase Mac computers. ☐ Yes ☐ No	
4. Which of the following Federal programs do you feel is the most effective in assisting students to succeed? (choose only one) ☐ NCLB ☐ SES ☐ ME ☐ FSS ☐ EETT ☐ ESLL	
5. How do you feel about the instructor(s) of this course? ________________________________	

(continued)

6. Which of the following is not an example of a non-example of a research method?

- ☐ Surveys
- ☐ Wikipedia
- ☐ Podcasts
- ☐ Slideshows

7. Which of the following are types of questions that can be used in surveys?

- ☐ Choice—One Answer (Vertical)
- ☐ Choice—One Answer (Horizontal)
- ☐ Choice—One Answer (Menu)
- ☐ Choice—Multiple Answers (Vertical)
- ☐ Choice—Multiple Answers (Horizontal)
- ☐ Matrix—One Answer per Row (Rating Scale)
- ☐ Matrix—Multiple Answers per Row
- ☐ Matrix—Multiple Answers per Row (Menus)
- ☐ Open Ended—One Line w/Prompt
- ☐ Open Ended—One or More Lines w/Prompt
- ☐ Open Ended—Essay
- ☐ Open Ended—Constant Sum
- ☐ Open Ended—Date and/or Time
- ☐ Presentation—Descriptive Text
- ☐ Presentation—Image
- ☐ Presentation—Spacer

BEYOND THE NUMBERS 1.2

What's Simple about an SRS?

Name: ______________________ Section Number: ________

To be graded, all assignments must be completed and submitted on the original book page.

Background

The definition of a simple random sample (SRS) can be confusing: An SRS of size *n* is a sample of size *n*, chosen in such a way that all samples of size *n* have the same chance of being chosen. It doesn't help that the word "random" is used in many different ways, but when it comes to selecting a simple random sample, we have to be very careful to know its technical meaning. We will explore these issues in this set of activities.

EXHIBIT 1

Random Evolution

On November 30th, 2012, National Public Radio ran a short segment entitled "That's So Random: The Evolution of an Odd Word." You may find this segment at http://www.npr.org/2012/11/30/166240531/thats-so-random-the-evolution-of-an-odd-word.

Question

1. List two uses of the word "random" from the audio that are different from the technical definition given above. How do you use the term "random" in your own life?

EXHIBIT 2

Careful Counting

The audio segment ends with Charlie McDonnell (of the British "Fun Science" videos) noting that "every now and then, at random, you end up with something awesome." We might take that to mean that every now and then, a simple random sample is representative of a population with respect to a certain list of demographics. Let's look at a simple example to see how likely that might be. Suppose you have a population with two men—one a Republican and one a Democrat; and two women—one a Republican and one a Democrat.

Questions

1. List all possible distinct samples of size two from this four-person population. Make sure that your notation makes it possible to distinguish all four members of the population.

2. For a simple random sample of size two, all samples of size two have the same chance of being chosen. What would the likelihood be of choosing any one of these samples?

   $\frac{1}{6}$

3. Suppose for a sample of size two to be "representative" of the population, it has to have exactly one man and one woman, and one Democrat and one Republican. What is the chance of selecting a simple random sample of size two from this population that is representative (in this sense of the word)?

EXHIBIT 3

Social Media Sampling

Suppose you have 113 friends on Facebook and you want to choose a simple random sample of 20 of them. Answer the following:

Questions

1. What is your population?

2. Describe in detail how you would select your simple random sample.

BEYOND THE NUMBERS 1.3

Are Online Reviews Statistical Samples?

Name: ____ Section Number: ________

To be graded, all assignments must be completed and submitted on the original book page.

EXHIBIT 1

Bravos for Bucks

The VIP brand Kindle Fire cover received 4,945 reviews on Amazon by early 2012, averaging a nearly perfect 4.9 stars out of five. That's quite impressive. It is tempting to think that online reviews, especially those posted at major sites like Amazon, are representative of consumer experiences. We know, however, that voluntary responses are often biased. But are product reviews even less accurate than previously thought? In his 2012 *Time* article "9 Reasons Why You Shouldn't Trust Online Reviews," Brad Tuttle writes, "You shouldn't believe everything you read. And if you're reading online reviews of products, hotels, restaurants, or local businesses or services? Then you should believe even less." You can find Tuttle's article online at http://business.time.com/2012/02/03/9-reasons-why-you-shouldnt-trust-online-reviews/.

Questions

1. Describe three reasons listed in the article as to why you should be very cautious about online reviews.

2. What was VIP doing to boost the ratings of its Kindle Fire cover? Be specific.

3. Compared to computer algorithms, how well did people perform in spotting fake reviews? How does this study inform your perception of online reviews?

BEYOND THE NUMBERS 1.4

Random or Representative?

Name: ______________________________ Section Number: ________

To be graded, all assignments must be completed and submitted on the original book page.

EXHIBIT 1

Gulliver Travels

900 people live in Gulliver, a small town in Michigan's Upper Peninsula.[1] You want to know what proportion of Gulliver's population supports legalizing marijuana. Suppose you already know the following demographic information about Gulliver's 900 citizens:

Gender
500 are Females

Income	20% make more than $80,000		70% make between $40,000 and $80,000		10% make less than $40,000	
Political Affilliation	70% Democrat	30% Republican	50% Democrat	50% Republican	30% Democrat	70% Republican

Gender
400 are Males

Income	40% make more than $80,000		50% make between $40,000 and $80,000		10% make less than $40,000	
Political Affilliation	60% Democrat	40% Republican	50% Democrat	50% Republican	40% Democrat	60% Republican

Questions

1. You have enough money to interview 90 residents. Working much the way Gallup did in the 1930s, you want your sample of 90 to mirror the distribution of subjects in the population exactly (at least along the lines of gender, income, and political affiliation). How many people would your sample place in the groups shown on the next page? If a calculation results in a partial person (e.g., 6.4 persons), leave the number as it is—don't round.

[1] There really is a Gulliver, MI, of about this size. The demographics are completely made up, however.

TABLE 1.1 Population Data

Category	Number of Persons
Males	
Females	
Males making between \$40,000 and \$80,000 yearly	
Females making less than \$40,000 per year who are Democrats	
Male Republicans making over \$80,000 per year	

2. Suppose the cross-sectional sample taken above represents a perfect microcosm of the larger population with respect to the legalization of marijuana. Is there any uncertainty involved in using this sample to represent the proportion of people in Gulliver who favor the legalization of marijuana? Explain.

3. Suppose you decided, instead, to take a simple random sample of Gulliver's population. Explain how you could take an SRS of size 90 from this population.

4. A carefully chosen simple random sample may not be representative of the population. Explain how this could be.

BEYOND THE NUMBERS 1.5

Research Randomizer

Name: ____ Section Number: ________

To be graded, all assignments must be completed and submitted on the original book page.

Background

A simple random sample is the easiest kind of statistically viable sample to select and measure. But how do you actually select an SRS? One useful tool is the Research Randomizer, available at http://www.randomizer.org/. The following activities are designed to allow you to get familiar with this tool.

EXHIBIT 1

No-Stumble Sampling

Data from the NHTSA's 1998 San Diego field sobriety test validation study is available at statconcepts.com/student-resources/sta-296-datasets. There are 296 participants in this study, so there are 296 case numbers displayed. Note, though, that these case numbers do not run sequentially from 1 to 296. Your job is to use Research Randomizer to select a sample of 20 cases from this data set.

Questions

1. Explain how you plan to identify the cases for Research Randomizer

2. What entries did you use for the following Research Randomizer fields?

TABLE 1.2 Research Randomizer Fields

How many sets of numbers do you want to generate?	How many numbers per set?	Number Range (e.g., 1–50)

3. For the 20 cases selected, fill out the following chart:

TABLE 1.3 Results for 20 Cases

Case Number	Actual BAC	Case Number	Actual BAC

4. What is the average BAC ("Blood Alcohol Content") of the 20 selected cases?

5. What proportion of cases in your sample had BACs at or above the legal limit of 0.04?

EXHIBIT 2

Social Media Sampling Revisited

Suppose you have 113 friends on Facebook and you want to choose a simple random sample of 20 of them to ask a survey question you have constructed.

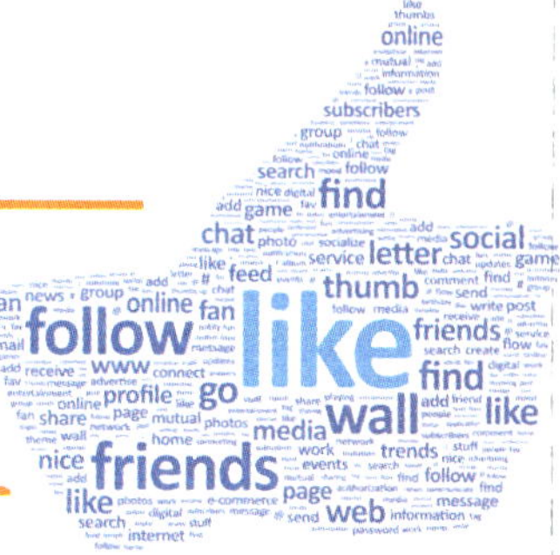

Question

1. Carefully explain how you could use Research Randomizer to select your sample.

BEYOND THE NUMBERS 1.6

How Do National Polls Sample?

Name: Laney Ratterman Section Number: ________

To be graded, all assignments must be completed and submitted on the original book page.

EXHIBIT 1

Getting Gallup

The following is an excerpt from Gallup's website describing their Daily Tracking Survey. The page is available at http://www.gallup.com/174155/gallup-daily-tracking-methodology.aspx.

> Gallup interviews U.S. adults aged 18 and older living in all 50 states and the District of Columbia using a dual-frame design, which includes both landline and cellphone numbers. Gallup samples landline and cell phone numbers using random-digit-dial methods. Gallup purchases samples for this study from Survey Sampling International (SSI). Gallup chooses landline respondents at random within each household based on which member had the next birthday. Each sample of national adults includes a minimum quota of 50% cellphone respondents and 50% landline respondents, with additional minimum quotas by time zone within region. Gallup conducts interviews in Spanish for respondents who are primarily Spanish-speaking.

Questions

1. What is the actual population being addressed by a Gallup telephone survey? Be very precise with your answer.

   Adults living in all 50 states and D.C. where half use a cell phone and half use a landline.

2. In what sense can a random-digit-dial sample be thought of as a simple random sample? Be very specific. It can be thought of as a simple random sample because technology is used to select participants [illegible] a landline can be chosen. The numbers are generated at random.

EXHIBIT 2

Weighting Room

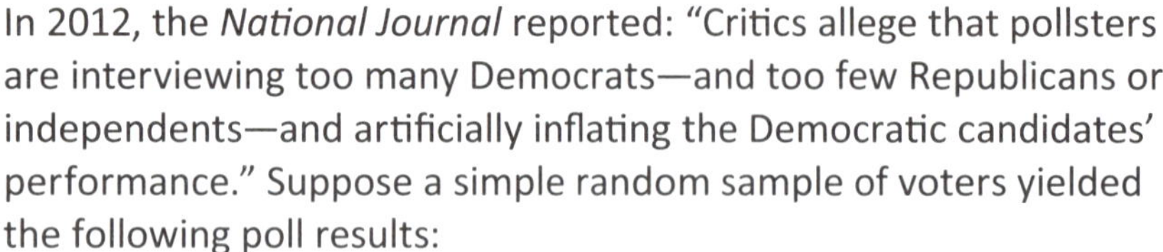

In 2012, the *National Journal* reported: "Critics allege that pollsters are interviewing too many Democrats—and too few Republicans or independents—and artificially inflating the Democratic candidates' performance." Suppose a simple random sample of voters yielded the following poll results:

TABLE 1.4 Poll Results

Results of a Random Sample of 100 Likely Voters	Planned to Vote "Obama"	Planned to Vote "Romney"
80 Democrats	70%	30%
20 Republicans	20%	80%

Questions

1. What proportion of likely voters overall (Democrats and Republicans combined) planned to vote for Barack Obama?

→ 60%

2. Do you think the proportion you provided above is an underestimate or an overestimate? How do your findings relate to the claim made in the *National Journal*?

I think that this is an overestimate because there were more [illegible] than republicans in the sample. My findings agree with the National Journal

3. Suppose that in the larger population, half of all likely voters are Democrats and half are Republicans. Now imagine that our simple random sample was comprised of 50 Democrats and 50 Republicans (instead of 80 Democrats and 20 Republicans). Re-compute the proportion of likely voters who planned to vote for Barack Obama. What percent decrease is this from the computation you did for Question 1?[2]

45% → 15% decrease

[2] Polling organizations often reweight in a similar, but more complicated, manner to better fit known population demographics. However, weighting election polls by party identification is very controversial because of the uncertainty in actual voter turnout.

BEYOND THE NUMBERS 1.7

Non-Sampling Errors: The Elephant in the Room

Name: ______________________________ Section Number: ________

To be graded, all assignments must be completed and submitted on the original book page.

Healthcare Reform

Title: Many Americans Still Confused about New Healthcare Reform Law and Its Provisions

Source: Harris Interactive, July 29, 2010, http://www.prnewswire.com/news-releases/many-americans-still-confused-about-new-healthcare-reform-law-and-its-provisions-99541539.html

Harris Interactive is a huge polling organization. Not too long ago, it took the unprecedented step of including a disclaimer at the end of its surveys. The article below offers an example.

> Not sure what's in—and not in—the new healthcare legislation signed into law by President Barack Obama in March? You're not alone. More than 2,100 adults were given a list of 18 reform items and asked to identify what's included and what's not included in the law. Only four items were correctly identified by the majority of those polled.
>
> Most (58%) know that the reform package will prohibit insurers from denying coverage to people because they are already sick; 55% know the law permits children to stay on their parents' insurance plan until age 26; and 52% realize that people who don't have insurance will be subject to financial penalties. Additionally, half are aware that employers with more than 50 employees will have to offer their workers affordable insurance. ...
>
> **Methodology** This survey was conducted online within the United States July 15 to 19, 2010 among 2,104 adults (aged 18 and over). Figures for age, sex, race/ethnicity, education, region, and household income were weighted where necessary to bring them into line with their actual proportions in the population. Propensity score weighting was also used to adjust for respondents' propensity to be online.
>
> All sample surveys and polls, whether or not they use probability sampling, are subject to multiple sources of error which are most often not possible to quantify or estimate, including sampling error, coverage error, error associated with nonresponse, error associated with question wording and response options, and post-survey weighting and adjustments. Therefore, Harris Interactive avoids the words "margin of error" as they are misleading. All that can be calculated are different possible sampling errors with different probabilities for pure, unweighted, random samples with 100% response rates. These are only theoretical because no published polls come close to this ideal.
>
> Respondents for this survey were selected from among those who have agreed to participate in Harris Interactive surveys. The data have been weighted to reflect the composition of the adult population. Because the sample is based on those who agreed to participate in the Harris Interactive panel, no estimates of theoretical sampling error can be calculated.
>
> Full data available at www.harrisinteractive.com. The results of this Harris Poll may not be used in advertising, marketing or promotion without the prior written permission of Harris Interactive.
>
> *These statements conform to the principles of disclosure of the National Council on Public Polls.*

In November 2013, Harris Interactive was purchased by Nielsen, and now publishes as The Harris Poll. The same disclaimer about the margin of error is still being used.

Questions

1. Follow your instructor's instructions to find a 95% and an 80% margin of error for the true proportion of all Americans who believe that the reform package will prohibit insurers from denying coverage to people.

2. What is meant by the following two statements that appear in the Methodology section? Offer a very clear explanation for each.

   a. "Therefore, Harris Interactive avoids the words 'margin of error' as they are misleading."

   b. "Because the sample is based on those who agreed to participate in the Harris Interactive panel, no estimates of theoretical sampling error can be calculated."

3. Which type of error does the Harris Poll seem to be claiming is the most difficult to get a handle on?

THEME 2

Experimentation

BEYOND THE NUMBERS 2.1

Slippery Evidence and Confounding

Name: Laney Ratterman Section Number: 009

To be graded, all assignments must be completed and submitted on the original book page.

Carefully read and think about each of the exhibits below. Then, give detailed answers to the questions that accompany each exhibit.

EXHIBIT 1

Questions

1. Looking at the Results section, what conclusion are you likely to make about the effectiveness of online instruction?

online instruction is just as effective as in-person instruction

Thinking Critically

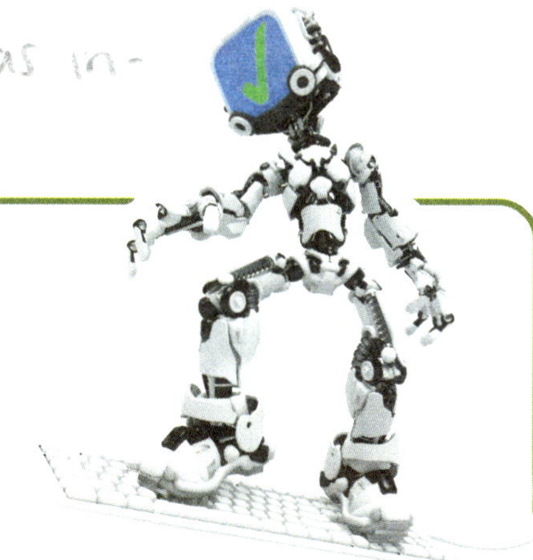

Title: Learning in an Online Format versus an In-Class Format: An Experimental Study

Authors: Allan H. Schulman and Randi L. Sims

Source: *T.H.E. Journal* 26, no. 11 (1999): 54–56

Methodology Students enrolled in five different undergraduate online courses during the Fall semester 1997 participated in a voluntary test-retest study designed to measure their learning of the course material. These students were compared with students enrolled in traditional in-class courses taught by the same instructors.

Subjects In total, 40 undergraduate students were enrolled in the online courses and 59 undergraduate students were enrolled in the in-class courses during the testing period.

Pre-tests Instructors designed pre-tests to measure the level of knowledge students had of the course content prior to the start of the course. The average pre-test scores for online students was 40.70 (s.d. = 24.03). The average pre-test scores for in-class students was 27.64 (s.d. = 21.62).

Post-tests Instructors designed post-tests on a 100-point scale to test students' knowledge at the end of the course. The average post-test scores for online students was 77.80 (s.d. = 18.64). The average post-test scores for in-class students was 77.58 (s.d. = 16.93).

Results [O]ur results indicate that there were no significant differences for post-test scores. ...

2. Give at least two reasons why this conclusion might be compromised. Be sure your reasons come from the part of this paper that you have access to here.

There were more students enrolled in the in-person class than the online ones which could skew the numbers.

There was a large difference between the pre-test scores for online and in-class students.

① No randomization to the online + in-class group

② Difference in pretest scores

EXHIBIT 2

"Make Mine a Large"

In the 2009 *New York Times* piece "Excess Pounds, but Not Too Many, May Lead to Longer Life," author Roni Caryn Rabin reported:

> Being overweight won't kill you—it may even help you live longer. That's the latest from a study that analyzed data on 11,326 Canadian adults, ages 25 and older, who were followed over a 12-year period. The report ... found that overall, people who were overweight but not obese—defined as a body mass index of 25 to 29.9—were actually less likely to die than people of normal weight, defined as a B.M.I. of 18.5 to 24.9.
>
> By contrast, people who were underweight, with a B.M.I. under 18.5, were more likely to die than those of average weight. Their risk of dying was 73% higher than that of normal weight people.

Question

1. Although this article doesn't describe an experiment, it does imply that being a little overweight may lead to a longer life. Identify at least one confounding variable that may compromise the validity of this inference. Support your case.

Wealth, because people with more money can afford more food making them more likely to be overweight

BMI is a measure of body fat and weight + it is not a good measure to see if people live longer.

confounding variable: health [illegible]

BEYOND THE NUMBERS 2.2

Experimentation Takes Flight

Name: ______________________________ Section Number: ________

To be graded, all assignments must be completed and submitted on the original book page.

Carefully read and think about each of the exhibits below. Then, give detailed answers to the questions that appear at the very end.

EXHIBIT 1

Plane Talk

Following your instructor's lead, the class will be divided into two groups denoted as Group A and Group B. Members of Group A will build the paper airplane *Design A*. Members of Group B will build the paper airplane *Design B*.

DESIGN A

1. First, fold the sheet in half lengthwise along the center line. Open the sheet out again.
2. Fold the two top corners down and in to meet the center line.
3. Fold the sheet in half widthwise, making the tip meet the base at the center fold. Fold flaps A and B up and in so the edges that used to be at the bottom meet in the center.
4. Fold along the dotted lines as shown to create an airplane resembling the one in the final step.
5. Finally, staple as shown, if a stapler is available.

A
B
staple here

DESIGN B

1. First, fold the sheet in half lengthwise.
2. Fold the short edge of one side down to the first fold, producing a 45 degree angle. Repeat this step on the other side of the original fold.
3. Fold the edge you created in the second step down to the original fold. Again, repeat this on the other side.
4. Once again, fold the newly created edges down on both sides to meet the original fold.
5. Hold the original crease at center and open the plane's wings out.

Hold center and fold wings out

EXHIBIT 2

Ready for Takeoff

Planes will be flown per instructor's directions. The linear distance traveled will be measured. This can be done very precisely or can be done in a clever and quick way (for example, the number of tiles or stairs passed). Your instructor will explain what she wants.

Record the 20 measurements below and compute the averages of each.

Airplane Type A Design Distance Traveled	Airplane Type B Design Distance Traveled
Average:	Average:

Questions

1. Identify the explanatory and response variables in this experiment.

2. Identify at least one potential source of confounding and suggest how it might be rectified.

3. Look at the two sets of 10 data points and their averages. Is there a difference due to design? Elaborate.

BEYOND THE NUMBERS 2.3

Questionable Evidence

Name: ____ Section Number: _______

To be graded, all assignments must be completed and submitted on the original book page.

EXHIBIT 1

Cancer Carafe

On March 12, 1981, the *New York Times* reported on a Harvard study that linked coffee consumption and pancreatic cancer. Article author Harold Schmeck Jr. noted that "[t]he report estimated that more than half of the pancreatic cancer cases that occurred in the United States might be attributable to coffee drinking ...." To complete the assignment, begin by reading Schmeck's article: http://www.nytimes.com/1981/03/12/us/study-links-coffee-use-to-pancreas-cancer.html. If this link does not work, search for the article under its title "Study Links Coffee Use to Pancreas Cancer," or by its author.

Questions

1. What two groups were being compared in this experiment?

2. List at least two other sources of circumstantial evidence that were cited in the article as further support of a link between pancreatic cancer and coffee.

3. Schmeck followed up on this article with another one titled "Critics Say Coffee Study Was Flawed." List three potential sources of confounding mentioned in this article and comment on why these could potentially destroy any claim to cause and effect? You can find the article online at: http://www.nytimes.com/1981/06/30/science/critics-say-coffee-study-was-flawed.html?module=Search&mabReward=relbias%3Ar. Use the space on the next page, if needed, to complete your answer.

EXHIBIT 2

Of Mice and People

Read the article "Misleading Mouse Studies Waste Medical Resources" by Erika Hayden, which appeared in *Nature* on March 26, 2014. You may find it at http://www.nature.com/news/misleading-mouse-studies-waste-medical-resources-1.14938.

Questions

1. The article addresses amyotrophic lateral sclerosis (ALS), suggesting that mice studies might be misleading. The article gives two reasons why. List both of those here.

2. A 1958 amendment to the Food, Drugs, and Cosmetic Act of 1938 called the "Delaney Clause" has been instrumental in the banning of food additives since its enactment. Find and state the exact text of the one-sentence Delaney Clause.

3. In February 2014, sandwich giant Subway announced it would stop using azodicarbonamide in its breads. Research this decision and comment on the indirect role that the Delaney Amendment had in Subway's decision. You may be able to find CNN article by Elizabeth Landau about this issue at: http://www.cnn.com/2014/02/06/health/subway-bread-chemical/.

4. Do you believe that misleading studies can still be beneficial to society? If so, explain some potential benefits of misleading studies. If not, explain what can be done to limit the number of misleading studies that are conducted.

BEYOND THE NUMBERS 2.4

Random Reflections

Name: Laney Ratterman ______ Section Number: ______

To be graded, all assignments must be completed and submitted on the original book page.

EXHIBIT 1

What's Random

It is easy to confuse different sources of randomization and the reasons as to why each is important to experimentation. The following table lists the likely effect when random assignment is used (or not) and random sampling is used (or not). Six entries have been left out of the table and scrambled in the list below. Match the effect descriptions to their corresponding letters in the table.

	Descriptions	Letter
1.	Confounding not addressed; results generalize to population	B
2.	Experimental conclusions do not generalize to population	E
3.	Confounding not addressed; so weak claim for causation with results	F
4.	Confounding addressed; results generalize to population	A
5.	Experimental conclusions generalize to population	C
6.	Confounding addressed; results don't generalize beyond sample	D

TABLE 2.1 What's Random

	Random Assignment to Treatments	No Random Assignment to Treatments	
Subjects Randomly Sampled from Population	A	B	C
Subjects not Randomly Sampled from Population	D	Confounding not addressed; results don't generalize beyond sample	E
	Confounding addressed; so solid claim for causation with results	F	

EXHIBIT 2

Random Opposition

Not everyone thinks that random assignment is ethical or even sensible. That discussion is beyond the scope of our mission here, but it is instructive to consider a problem that was the topic of a debate in the 1920s between two prominent statisticians, Sir Ronald Fisher and William Gossett.[1]

Question

1. Suppose you have a field that is divided into 24 rectangular plots as shown below. Two crop varieties (A and B) are to be assigned to those 24 plots and their yields compared after a season. Research Randomizer© was used to make these random assignments. The result is shown to the right.

Suppose, also, that the ground decreases in fertility as you move from the river to the tree line. Nine of the twelve B varieties are in the lower two rows of plots, and nine of the twelve A varieties are in the upper two rows. Hence, B has a distinct advantage.

Design a decidedly non-random distribution of A and B that would effectively balance out any North-South *and* East-West variation in soil quality, sun exposure, etc. Enter your letters in the empty plot below. You should end up with 12 As and 12 Bs.

Support your design in the space below.

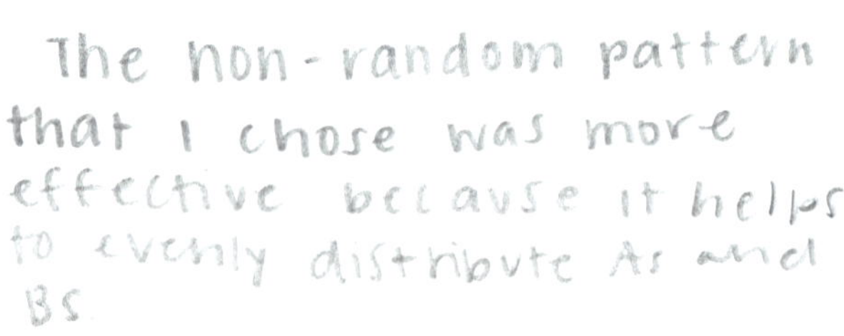

The non-random pattern that I chose was more effective because it helps to evenly distribute As and Bs.

[1] See "The Unprincipled Randomization Principle in Economics and Medicine," by Stephen T. Ziliak and Edward R. Teather-Posadas for more discussion, including a reflection on a recent randomized eyeglass experiment in China.

BEYOND THE NUMBERS 2.5

What to Believe?

Name: ____ Section Number: ________

To be graded, all assignments must be completed and submitted on the original book page.

Background

When it comes to experimentation, principled implementation and ethical reporting are obviously critical to the integrity of all associated human inference. Unfortunately, there are a surprisingly large number of cases where dishonesty or exploitation, not just carelessness or confounding, tainted or nullified the significance of the findings. You will investigate three examples of research misconduct in this activity.

EXHIBIT 1

Piltdown Meltdown—1912

In 1912, Charles Dawson discovered two skulls found in the Piltdown quarry in Sussex, England. These skulls were said to be from a primitive hominid and were hailed as the "missing link" between man and ape. Research the Piltdown Man and write a well-formed summary of what ultimately was revealed about the skulls. Give specific details about the nature of the deception that was uncovered. How does this case affect your understanding of statistics going forward?

EXHIBIT 2

Marker Mice—1974

William T. Summerlin used to work at Memorial Sloan Kettering Cancer Center in New York City, conducting research in transplantation immunology. His work could have had major implications for reducing the rejection rates of transplanted tissue. Research Dr. Summerlin and write a well-formed summary of what ultimately was revealed about his work. Give specific details about the nature of the deception that was uncovered. What caused Summerlin to behave as he did, and what can be done to avoid such deceptions?

EXHIBIT 3

Doing the Dishes—2010

Dr. Vipul Bhrigu was a researcher at the University of Michigan when he began to feel professionally threatened by the work of a graduate student in the same lab, Heather Ames. Desperate for his work not to be overshadowed, he concocted a plan to keep hers from moving ahead. Research Dr. Bhrigu and write a well-formed summary of what ultimately was revealed about his deception. Give specific details about the nature of the sabotage that was uncovered. How can this type of sabotage be avoided?

THEME 3

Two Quantitive Variables

BEYOND THE NUMBERS 3.1

Association and Causation

Name: Laney Ratterman Section Number: ________

To be graded, all assignments must be completed and submitted on the original book page.

Carefully read and think about each of the exhibits below. Then, give detailed answers to the questions that appear at the very end.

EXHIBIT 1

Breakfast and Biology

Title: Does Eating Breakfast Affect the Performance of College Students on Biology Exams?

Author: Gregory W. Phillips, Blinn College

Source: *Bioscience* 30, no. 4 (2005): 15–19

Abstract This study examined the breakfast eating habits of 1,259 college students over an eleven-year period to determine if eating breakfast had an impact upon their grade on a General Biology exam.

...

Results and Discussion This study showed that students who ate breakfast had a higher success rate on General Biology exams than those students who did not eat breakfast. This finding supports earlier research, which indicated that eating breakfast affects student performance.

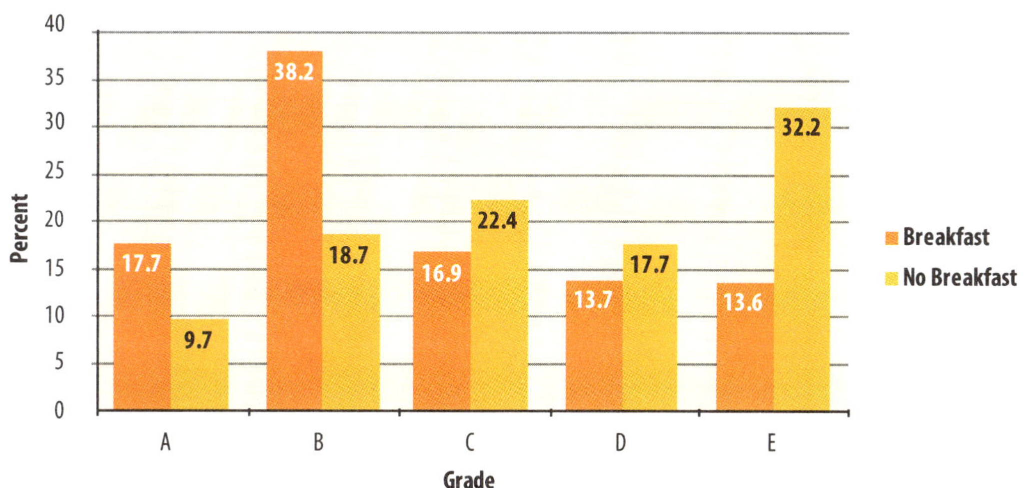

Source: Gregory W. Phillips "Does Eating Breakfast Affect the Performance of College Students on Biology Exams?" *Bioscience* 30, no. 4 (2005): 15–19.

Question

1. Based solely on the graph, could you say eating breakfast *affects* student performance? Explain.

No, you could not tell if breakfast solely affects student performance because there are other factors to consider.

EXHIBIT 2

Mortality and Global Warming

On November 14, 2007, the Kentucky legislature held hearings on global warming with speakers Christopher Walker Monckton and James Taylor of the Heartland Institute.

Look at the graph below, allegedly typical of the exhibits that Monckton and Taylor showed.

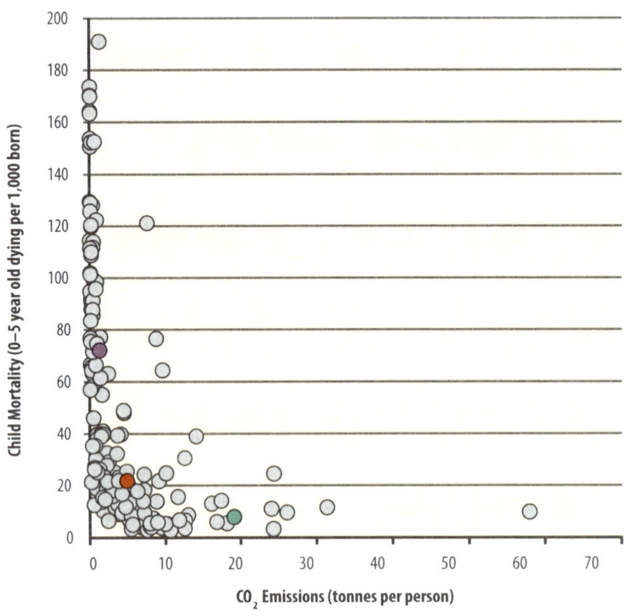

For example, India is the blue circle centered at 1.3 tonnes of CO_2 per person (*x*-value) and 72 child/infant deaths per 1,000 births (*y*-value). You should take a close look at the trend exhibited by the plot. The red circle represents China and the green circle represents the United States.

Question

1. Reportedly, the Legislature was told that this graph shows that global warming is good because it *causes* a decrease in infant mortality. Is this an accurate assessment? Explain.

No, like the other question, there are many other factors to consider. For example, countries with more wealth are more likely to produce higher levels of CO_2

BEYOND THE NUMBERS 3.2

Association and Causation Revisited

Name: ______________________________ Section Number: ________

To be graded, all assignments must be completed and submitted on the original book page.

EXHIBIT 1

Vaccines and Risk

Deadly Immunity

In 2005, *Salon* published an exclusive online story by Robert F. Kennedy, Jr, that offered an explosive premise. Kennedy proposed that the mercury-based thimerosal compound present in vaccines until 2001 was dangerous, and that he was "convinced that the link between thimerosal and the epidemic of childhood neurological disorders is real."

This article was co-published to a wide audience by way of *Rolling Stone* magazine. Mr. Kennedy based his conclusions on a number of sources, but in part on graphs like you see below. (DTP is diphtheria, tetanus, and pertussis.)

DTP Coverage and Autism Prevalence by Birth Year

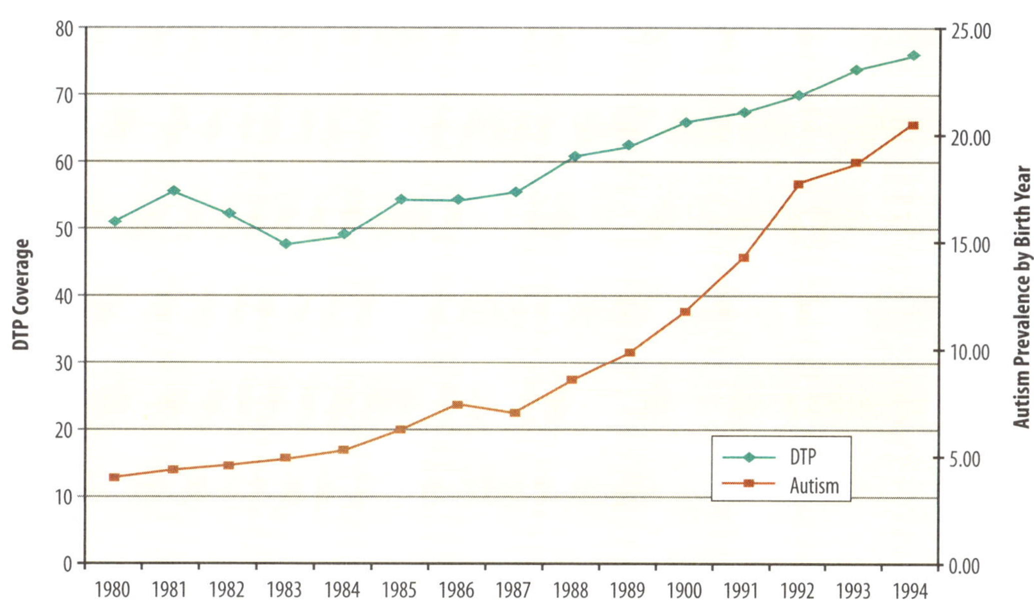

Source: "Data Obtained by MM Show There's No Association between DTP Vaccination and Autism," *Autism News Science and Opinion,* June 14, 2008, http://leftbrainrightbrain.co.uk/2008/06/data-obtained-by-mm-show-theres-no-association-between-dtp-vaccination-and-autism/.

Question

1. Is there any evidence from the graph of cause and effect? Explain.

EXHIBIT 2

Bran Flakes on My Doughnut

Title: Whole Grains Do a Heart Good

Author: Ed Edelson

Source: HealthDay News, Monday October 22, 2007, http://www.washingtonpost.com/wp-dyn/content/article/2007/10/22/AR2007102201449.html

Diets rich in whole grains, fruits, vegetables, and even a little alcohol may help ward off heart woes, new studies show. In one study, regular consumption of whole-grain breakfast cereal cut the risk of heart failure for male American physicians.

Compared to those who ate no whole-grain cereal, men who consumed two to six servings per week saw their risk of heart failure fall by 21%, while those who ate seven or more servings per week reaped a 29% reduction in risk, the researchers reported in the October 22 issue of the *Archives of Internal Medicine*.

Question

1. Does this study suggest that eating whole-grain cereal is associated with heart failure risk? If so, what is the nature of the suggested association? Is there evidence of causation? Explain.

BEYOND THE NUMBERS 3.3

Scatterplots—Part I

Name: Laney Ratterman Section Number: ________

To be graded, all assignments must be completed and submitted on the original book page.

EXHIBIT 1

Anscombe's Activity

These data were created by F.J. Anscombe[1] in 1973 to remind us of the importance of plotting our data. You will see these data again later in this workbook.

Questions

1. Create a scatterplot of *y*1 versus *x*1 on the axes below. Does the plot show a positive association or a negative association? How do you know?

   Positive - it is trending upwards

2. Create a scatterplot of *y*4 versus *x*4. Does the plot show a positive association or a negative association? How do you know? Make sure you turn in your plots with this assignment.

   positive - has a positive slope

TABLE 3.1 F.J. Anscombe's Data

Obs	x1	y1	x4	y4
1	10	8.04	8	6.58
2	8	6.95	8	5.76
3	13	7.58	8	7.71
4	9	8.81	8	8.84
5	11	8.33	8	8.47
7	6	7.24	8	5.25
6	14	9.96	8	7.04
8	4	4.26	19	12.5
9	12	10.84	8	5.56
10	7	4.82	8	7.91
11	5	5.68	8	6.89

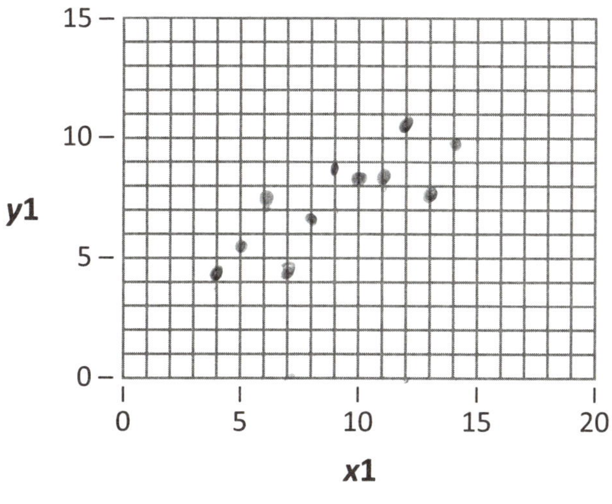

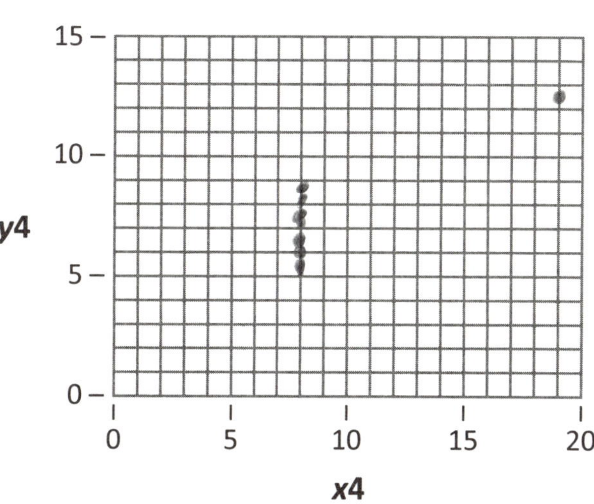

[1] Edward R. Tufte, The Visual Display of Quantitative Information (Cheshire, Connecticut: Graphics Press, 1983), pp. 14–15. F.J. Anscombe, "Graphs in Statistical Analysis," *American Statistician*, vol. 27 (Feb 1973), pp. 17–21.

EXHIBIT 2

Vaccines and Risk

There is an on-going debate regarding possible links between vaccines containing thimerosal and the onset of autism. The data set below lists the percentages of California children who received 4 doses of DTP by their second birthday and the number of autism cases logged in California's Department of Developmental Services' regional service center system.[2]

California 1980–1994

Autism Cases: 0, 200, 400, 600, 800, 1,000, 1,200, 1,400

DTP Coverage (%): 40, 50, 60, 70, 80

TABLE 3.2 California 1980–1994

Year	DTP Coverage (%)	Number of Autism Cases
1980	50.9	176
1981	55.4	201
1982	52.1	212
1983	47.7	229
1984	48.9	246
1985	54.3	293
1986	54.1	357
1987	55.3	347
1988	60.9	436
1989	62.2	522
1990	65.9	663
1991	67.3	823
1992	69.8	1,042
1993	73.6	1,090
1994	75.7	1,182

Questions

1. Create a scatterplot of Autism Cases versus DTP Coverage. Does the plot show a positive association or a negative association? How do you know? Make sure you submit your plot with this assignment.

positive – the line of regression has a positive slope

2. Is the association weak or strong? Defend your reasoning.

strong – most of the points fall pretty close to the line of regression

3. Should parents take these data into consideration when deciding whether to vaccinate their children? Defend your reasoning.

No - the vaccine wouldn't be the sol

[2] Dr. Loring Dales from the Immunization Branch of the California Department of Health Service made these data publically available at: http://www.putchildrenfirst.org/media/4.6.pdf. See also http://ncbi.nlm.nih.gov/pubmed/11231748.

BEYOND THE NUMBERS 3.4

Scatterplots—Part II

Name: ______________________________________ Section Number: ________

To be graded, all assignments must be completed and submitted on the original book page.

EXHIBIT 1

Mortality and Global Warming

In this exercise, you will construct a scatterplot of "Child Mortality" versus "CO_2 Emissions" for 191 countries, using 2006 data archived by Dr. Hans Rosling.[3] These data are available at statconcepts.com/student-resources/sta-296-datasets. Use an online applet or software package such as StatKey, Microsoft Excel, or Apple Numbers. Your instructor will tell you which package to use if a particular one is required. Make sure you label your axes and provide a professional plot. Answer the questions below. Save your computer work—you may need it for another Beyond the Numbers later on.

Questions

1. Construct your plot as instructed above. What software did you use? Make sure you submit your plot with this assignment.

2. Does the scatterplot show a positive association or a negative association? How do you know?

3. Is the association weak or strong? Defend your reasoning.

[3] Hans Rosling is Professor of International Health at Karolinska Institute and the co-founder and chairman of the Gapminder Foundation. Dr. Rosling is commited to making important public data available for easy plotting and analysis with his Gapminder software.

EXHIBIT 2

Mortality and Global Warming Transformed

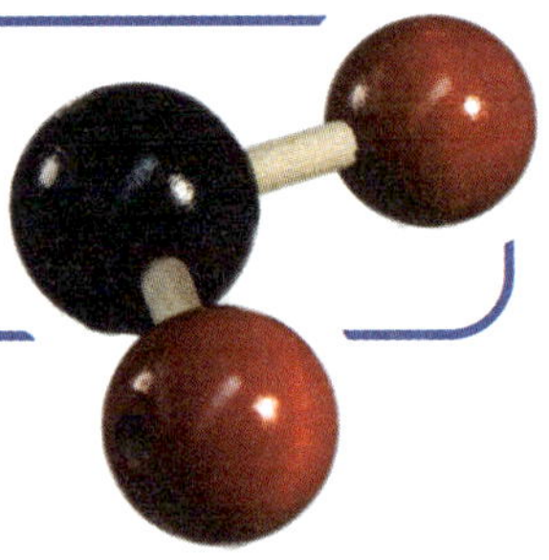

Save your computer work for this Exhibit. You may need it for another Beyond the Numbers later on.

Questions

1. Redo the scatterplot from Exhibit 1. Same rules as before: use a computer package and submit professional-level results. This time, plot $\log_{10}$ (Child Mortality) versus $\log_{10}$ (CO_2 Emissions). How does this plot compare to the one you did in Exhibit 1? Make sure you submit your plot with this assignment.

2. Does the scatterplot show a positive association or a negative association? How do you know?

3. Is the association weak or strong? Defend your reasoning.

4. Do these data affect how you feel about global warming? Why or why not?

BEYOND THE NUMBERS 3.5

Computing Correlations—Part I

Name: Laney Ratterman Section Number: 009

To be graded, all assignments must be completed and submitted on the original book page.

EXHIBIT 1

Anscombe's Activity Revisited

Recall Anscombe's data from Beyond the Numbers 3.3. In this activity, you will be asked to compute the correlation coefficient for each pair of variables and compare.

Questions

1. Compute r for the $(x1,y1)$ pairs.

   0.815

2. Compute r for the $(x4,y4)$ pairs.

   0.815

3. Compare the two r values you found in light of the scatterplots of these data (which you plotted earlier). What note of inferential caution does this exercise sound?

   correlation does not imply causation

TABLE 3.3 F.J. Anscombe's Data for $x1$ and $y1$

Obs	x1	y1	x1y1	$x1^2$	$y1^2$
1	10	8.04			
2	8	6.95			
3	13	7.58			
4	9	8.81			
5	11	8.33			
6	14	9.96			
7	6	7.24			
8	4	4.26			
9	12	10.84			
10	7	4.82			
11	5	5.68			
	$\Sigma x =$	$\Sigma y =$	$\Sigma xy =$	$\Sigma x^2 =$	$\Sigma y^2 =$

TABLE 3.4 F.J. Anscombe's Data for $x4$ and $y4$

Obs	x4	y4	x4y4	$x4^2$	$y4^2$
1	8	6.58			
2	8	5.76			
3	8	7.71			
4	8	8.84			
5	8	8.47			
6	8	7.04			
7	8	5.25			
8	19	12.5			
9	8	5.56			
10	8	7.91			
11	8	6.89			
	$\Sigma x =$	$\Sigma y =$	$\Sigma xy =$	$\Sigma x^2 =$	$\Sigma y^2 =$

EXHIBIT 2

Vaccines and Risk Revisited

Dr. Loring Dales of the Immunization Branch of the California Department of Health Service writes, "here are the data we have on (a) percentages of California children who had received 4 doses of DTP by their 2nd birthday ... and (b) numbers of autism cases in California's Department of Developmental Services regional service center system ...."

Questions

1. Fill out all the entries in the table that are missing. Your instructor may have you retype the table if you are not required to turn in this actual page.

2. Compute the correlation coefficient between DTP Coverage and Autism Prevalence.

   0.96166

TABLE 3.5 California 1980–1994 Data for *x* and *y*

Year	DTP Coverage (%)	Number of Autism Cases	*xy*	x^2	y^2
1980	50.9	176	8958.4	2590.8	30976
1981	55.4	201	11135	3069.2	40401
1982	52.1	212	11045	2714.4	44944
1983	47.7	229	10923	2275.3	52441
1984	48.9	246	12029	2391.2	60516
1985	54.3	293	15910	2948.5	85849
1986	54.1	357	19314	2926.8	127449
1987	55.3	347	19189	3058.1	120409
1988	60.9	436	26552	3708.8	190096
1989	62.2	522	32468	3868.8	272484
1990	65.9	663	43692	4342.8	439569
1991	67.3	823	55388	4529.3	677329
1992	69.8	1,042	72732	4872	
1993	73.6	1,090	80224	5417	
1994	75.7	1,182	89477	5730.5	
	$\Sigma x =$ 894.1	$\Sigma y =$ 7819	$\Sigma xy =$ 509038	$\Sigma x^2 =$ 54448	$\Sigma y^2 =$ 5813451

3. Has this exercise changed your perception of the data presented in Beyond the Numbers 3.3? Why or why not?

   No, the correlation is very strong but it still doesn't mean that correlation implies causation

BEYOND THE NUMBERS 3.6

Computing Correlations—Part II

Name: ______________________________ Section Number: ________

To be graded, all assignments must be completed and submitted on the original book page.

EXHIBIT 1

Mortality and Global Warming Revisited

Refer to Beyond the Numbers 3.4 Scatterplots—Part II. Hans Rosling is a professor of international health at Karolinska Institute and is the co-founder and chairman of the Gapminder Foundation. Dr. Rosling is committed to making important public data available for easy plotting and analysis with his Gapminder software.

In this exercise, you will compute the correlation coefficient between "Child Mortality" versus "CO_2 Emissions" for 192 countries using 2006 data archived by Dr. Rosling. These data are available at statconcepts.com/student-resources/sta-296-datasets. You must use an online applet or a software package such as StatKey, Microsoft Excel, or Apple Numbers. Your instructor will tell you which package to use if a particular one is required.

Questions

1. What is the value of *r*?

2. Does the value of *r* suggest the association between Child Mortality and CO_2 Emissions is strong or weak? How do you know?

3. Do you think the computation of *r* is appropriate for these data? Why or why not? (You constructed a scatterplot of these data in Beyond the Numbers 3.4.)

EXHIBIT 2

Transformations Revisited

Refer to Beyond the Numbers 3.4 Scatterplots—Part II. In this exercise, you will compute the correlation coefficient between $\log_{10}$ (Child Mortality) and $\log_{10}$ (CO_2 Emissions) for the 191 countries using 2006 data archived by Dr. Rosling. The raw data are available at statconcepts.com/student-resources/sta-296-datasets. You must use an online applet or a software package such as StatKey, Microsoft Excel, or Apple Numbers. Your instructor will tell you which package to use if a particular one is required.

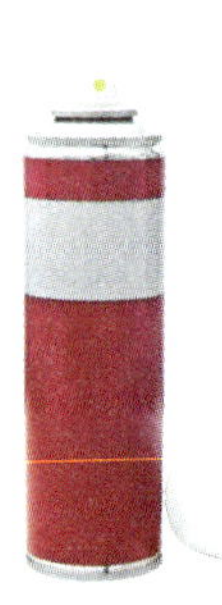

Questions

1. What is the value of *r*?

2. How does this value of *r* compare to the one found in Exhibit 1?

3. Does the value of *r* suggest the association between Child Mortality and CO_2 Emissions is strong or weak? How do you know?

4. Do you think the computation of *r* is appropriate for these data? Why or why not? (You constructed a scatterplot of these data in Beyond the Numbers 3.4.)

BEYOND THE NUMBERS 3.7

Outliers and Leverage Points

Name: Laney Ratterman Section Number: 009

To be graded, all assignments must be completed and submitted on the original book page.

EXHIBIT 1

Heptathletes

Finish data for two 1992 Olympic Heptathlon events are shown below. A scatterplot of the data is shown just to the left of the table. Chouaa is the green data point and Barber is the red one.

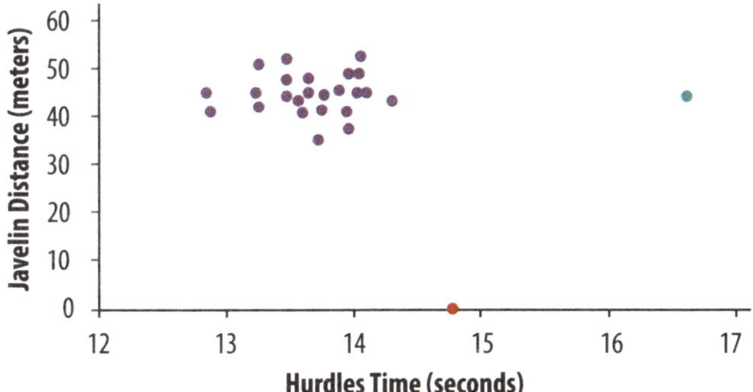

TABLE 3.6 Heptathletes

Name	Hurdles (seconds)	Javelin (meters)
Joyner-Kersee	12.85	44.98
Nastase	12.86	41.3
Dimitrova	13.23	44.48
Belova	13.25	41.9
Braun	13.25	51.12
Beer	13.48	48.1
Court	13.48	52.12
Kamrowska	13.48	44.12
Wlodarczyk	13.57	43.46
Greiner	13.59	40.78
Kaljurand	13.64	47.42
Zhu	13.64	45.12
Skjaeveland	13.73	35.42
Lesage	13.75	41.28
Nazaroviene	13.75	44.42
Aro	13.87	45.42
Marxer	13.94	41.08
Rattya	13.96	49.02
Carter	13.97	37.58
Atroshchenko	14.03	45.18
Vaidianu	14.04	49
Teppe	14.06	52.58
Clarius	14.1	45.14
Bond-Mills	14.31	43.3
Barber	14.79	0
Chouaa	16.62	44.4

Questions

1. What kind of association do you see in the scatterplot—positive, negative, neither? Support your answer.

Neither because there doesn't seem to be any relationship between the two variables.

2. Compute the correlation coefficient "*r*" for the entire data set. You should use a software package or an online applet as required by your instructor. Is this value of "*r*" consistent with what you answered in Question 1? Why or why not?

r = -0.2521 → negative association

It is not consistent with my answer because I said that the variables were not associated.

EXHIBIT 2

Language

In a scatterplot, outliers are data pairs that are not spatially close to the bulk of the data. Outliers are not necessarily a problem for the human inferences that arise from a correlation coefficient. However, if the removal of a single outlier causes a distinct change in the correlation, then that outlier is called an influence point. Influence points can disguise the essence of an association.

Questions

1. Looking at the scatterplot above, which athletes are outliers?

Barber and [illegible]

2. Compute the correlation coefficient "*r*" for the data set with Barber removed. Is Barber an influence point? Why?

T = 0.00066

Barber is an influence point because the correlation coefficient changed a lot [illegible] removal

3. Compare the value of "*r*" that you computed for the entire data set to the value of "*r*" that you computed with Barber removed. Which one best reflects the association seen in the scatterplot? Why?

The one with Barber removed because the "r" [illegible]

BEYOND THE NUMBERS 3.8

Simpson's Slippery Paradox

Name: ______________________________ Section Number: ________

To be graded, all assignments must be completed and submitted on the original book page.

EXHIBIT 1

Sex Discrimination at Berkeley

Title: Sex Bias in Graduate Admissions: Data from Berkeley

Author: P.J. Bickel, E.A. Hammel, and J. W. O'Connell

Source: *Science* 187, no. 4175 (1975): 398–404

Some years back, the University of Berkeley found evidence that there was sex discrimination in admission to graduate school. Tables 1.20, 1.21, and 1.22 represent data summarized from the original study.[4] In the following, think of Berkeley as divided into two colleges, College A and College B. Very oversimplified, granted, but it will make our point effectively.

Questions

1. Look at College A and compute the admission rates for men and women separately. What would you infer?

TABLE 3.7 College A

Gender	Not Admitted	Admitted	Totals
Men	520	865	1,385
Women	27	106	133

[4] The data from this study can be found in numerous places, including http://www.math.grinnell.edu/~mooret/reports/SimpsonExamples.pdf. Note that the original data have been rearranged, but this does not preclude us from drawing inferences about them.

2. Look at College B and compute the admission rates for men and women separately. What would you infer?

TABLE 3.8 College B

Gender	Not Admitted	Admitted	Totals
Men	973	333	1,306
Women	1251	451	1,702

3. In Table 3.9, we have combined both colleges. Explain how we get this table from the two above.

TABLE 3.9 Both Colleges Combined

Gender	Not Admitted	Admitted	Totals
Men	1493	1198	2,691
Women	1278	557	1,835

4. Look again at Table 3.9 and calculate the admission rates for men and women separately. What would you infer? Is this inference consistent with the ones you made in Questions 1 and 2? Explain.

THEME 4

Confidence Intervals

BEYOND THE NUMBERS 4.1

Mathematically Organic Bells

A Hands-On Approach

Name: Laney Ratterman Section Number: 009

To be graded, all assignments must be completed and submitted on the original book page.

Normal Development

Generating the Data

You instructor may conduct this experiment in a manner different from how it is written. He may use dice, spinners, Legos, magnetic strips, or objects completely other than those described below. The point of the exercise will be unchanged. It is a good exercise to do with a partner or in small groups, provided the actual number of samples generated is sufficiently large. Your instructor will clarify how he wants this done.

1. Roll your die 20 times and record the number of times an even face appears.
2. Using the conversion chart (Table 4.1) below, convert your results to a percentage and record that number here.

Percent of Even Faces: 50%

# of even

卌 卌

# of odd

卌 卌

TABLE 4.1

Number of Even Faces	Percentage of Even Faces	Number of Even Faces	Percentage of Even Faces
0	0	11	55
1	5	12	60
2	10	13	65
3	15	14	70
4	20	15	75
5	25	16	80
6	30	17	85
7	35	18	90
8	40	19	95
9	45	20	100
10	50		

A virtual version of this same exercise can be constructed using a spinner applet (e.g., http://www.shodor.org/interactivate/activities/BasicSpinner) and a histogram applet (e.g., http://www.shodor.org/interactivate/activities/Histogram/). Be aware that JAVA is now blocking unsigned applets. See https://www.java.com/en/download/help/java_blocked.xml for details and a confirmed workaround.

Displaying Your Result

Once you have calculated your percentage of even faces, come to the front of the room and place a magnetic strip in the category that corresponds to your sample percentage. (Your instructor may not use magnetic strips, as mentioned, but will demonstrate accordingly so you will know what to do.)

Questions

1. If you were to roll this die a really large number of times, about what percentage of even faces should you get?

   50%

2. What sort of real-world polling exercise could be modeled by this activity? Be sure to identify the population, sample, and statistic in that real polling context. → presidential (2 options)

   Any poll having to do with elections because there are 2 options meaning that the answers would be split close to 50/50 with a large sample size.

   population: all voters

   sample: voters that were polled

   statistic: around 0.50

3. After the structure is built, have a good look at it. What is its shape and where is the peak, more or less?

   Shape: bell curve

   Peak Is Above: 0.50

BEYOND THE NUMBERS 4.2

Confidence in Repetition

A Hands-On Approach

Name: ______________________________ Section Number: ________

To be graded, all assignments must be completed and submitted on the original book page.

Strip Searching for Meaning

Your instructor may facilitate this exercise in different ways. He may use dice, spinners, popsicle sticks, magnetic strips, or objects completely other than those described below. The point of the exercise will be unchanged. This is a good exercise to do with a partner or in small groups, provided the actual number of samples generated is sufficiently large. Your instructor will clarify how he wants this done in your class.

Generating the Data

To begin the exercise, please do the following:

1. Pair up with someone next to you. Each pair will receive one die. One member of your pair will roll the die 40 times while the other member records the number of times a 1, 2, 3, or 4 lands face up.
2. Switch roles, roll the die 40 more times, and record the outcomes. (It takes only about 3–5 minutes to roll a die a total of 80 times.)
3. Compute the proportion of the total 80 rolls that produced a 1, 2, 3, or 4. Keep good counts.
4. Record your sample proportion (out of 80 rolls) that came up 1, 2, 3, or 4: ____________

Displaying the Results

1. One person from each pair should come up front and take a long magnetic strip out of the collection of magnetic strips. Think of the center of this strip as the sample proportion you calculated. The strip represents a 95% confidence interval that is built around that sample proportion.
2. The other person from each pair should come up front and take a short magnetic strip out of the collection of magnetic strips. Think of the center of this strip as sample proportion you calculated. The strip represents an 80% confidence interval that is built around that sample proportion.
3. On the display board that your instructor has created, put the center of your magnetic strips, oriented horizontally, on the line that corresponds to the values of the sample proportions that you found.

A virtual version of this same exercise can be constructed using a spinner an applet (e.g., http://www.rossmanchance.com/applets/ConfSim.html). Be aware that JAVA is now blocking unsigned applets. See https://www.java.com/en/download/help/java_blocked.xml for details and a confirmed workaround.

(continued)

4. Keep the strip level with the floor and keep in mind that a lot of these strips may have to go on the display. Your instructor will demonstrate.
5. Record whether your strip overlaps the vertical line at ⅔: Yes ______ No ______. Your instructor will ask you to record this information for the class to see as well, perhaps by way of tick marks in a table or on a chart.

After everyone is finished, have a look at the class-wide display. It may be on the chalkboard or on a separate bulletin board.

Questions

1. What is the parameter and the population? Explain your answer.

2. About what percentage of the long strips overlap a vertical line through the parameter?

3. About what percentage of the short strips overlap a vertical line through the parameter?

4. Carefully articulate how "confident" you can be that a 95% confidence interval (one of the long strips) will contain the parameter?

BEYOND THE NUMBERS 4.3

A Challenging Interpretation

Name: ______________________________ Section Number: ________

To be graded, all assignments must be completed and submitted on the original book page.

Background

So far in this course you have not been introduced to the correct interpretation of a confidence interval. This activity will introduce you to the correct interpretation and common misinterpretations. The correct interpretation of a $K\%$ confidence interval based on a simple random sample of size n is as follows: about $K\%$ of all samples of size n will produce confidence intervals that contain the parameter.

EXHIBIT 1

A Common Problem

A team of psychology researchers[1] was interested in potential misinterpretations of the term "confidence" in a confidence interval. They collected data from 442 undergraduate students, 34 graduate students, and 118 of their research-active colleagues. All subjects were presented with a "fictitious scenario of a professor who conducts an experiment and reports a 95% CI for the [population proportion] that ranges from 0.1 to 0.4. Neither the topic of study nor the underlying statistical model used to compute the CI was specified in the survey." The subjects were then asked to specify whether they agreed or disagreed with each of the following statements as interpretations of that confidence interval (CI). Here is what the investigators found.

TABLE 4.2 Percentage of Subjects Agreeing with the Statement[1]

	Statement	First Year Students ($n = 442$)	Master Students ($n = 34$)	Researchers ($n = 118$)
1.	The probability that the true proportion is greater than 0 is at least 95%.	51%	32%	38%
2.	The probability that the true proportion equals 0 is smaller than 5%.	55%	44%	47%
3.	There is a 95% probability that the true proportion lies between 0.1 and 0.4.	58%	50%	59%
4.	We can be 95% confident that the true proportion lies between 0.1 and 0.4.	49%	50%	55%
5.	If we were to repeat the experiment over and over, then 95% of the time the true porportion falls between 0.1 and 0.4.	66%	79%	58%

[1] Hoekstra, R., Morey, R., Rouder, J., and Wagenmakers, E-J. "Robust misinterpretation of confidence intervals," *Psychon Bull Rev.* Published online January 14, 2014. http://www.ejwagenmakers.com/inpress/HoekstraEtAlPBR.pdf. Table has been reformatted, one statement omitted, and "mean" changed to "proportion" throughout.

All of the statements are wrong! Students and professional researchers alike found the interpretation of a confidence interval to be challenging. Yet, it is not acceptable to step away from this challenge. Confidence intervals are used everywhere as a kind of statistical seal of approval for survey and experiment results.

Questions

1. Identify which of these statements is acceptable for this course and explain what is missing from that statement.

2. Explain what is wrong with the other statements.

BEYOND THE NUMBERS 4.4

Get ME Out of the Way

Name: ______________________________ Section Number: ________

To be graded, all assignments must be completed and submitted on the original book page.

EXHIBIT 1

Texting Error

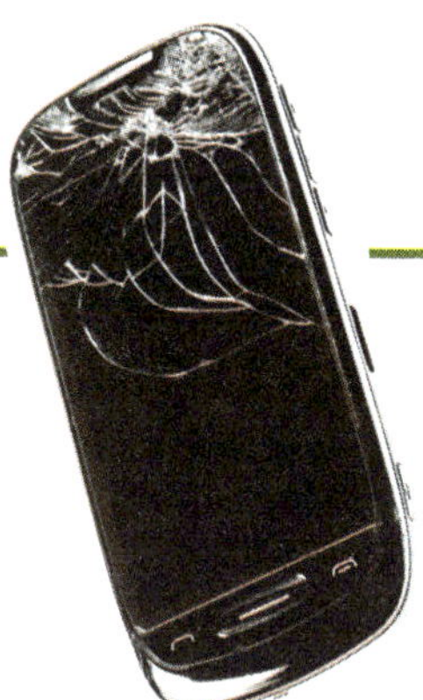

Title: Poll Finds Support for Ban on Texting at the Wheel

Author: Marjorie Connelly

Source: *New York Times*, September 27, 2009, http://www.nytimes.com/2009/09/28/technology/28truckerside.html

Read the following extract from the above article and answer the related questions to see if you understand the data.

> The public overwhelmingly supports the prohibition of text messaging while driving, the latest *New York Times*/CBS News Poll finds. Ninety percent of adults say sending a text message while driving should be illegal, and only 8% disagree.
>
> ...
>
> The *Times*/CBS News telephone poll was conducted September 19–23 with 1,042 adults nationwide and has a margin of sampling error of plus or minus three percentage points.

Questions

1. How was the sample taken and what was the result of the survey?

2. Suppose someone said to you, "Sure, of the 1,042 surveyed by the poll, 90% agreed, but I bet if you interviewed all American adults you would likely find only 50% agreeing!" Is 50% a plausible value for the entire population? Why or why not?

EXHIBIT 2

A Weak Majority

Title: Poll Finds Slim Majority Back More Afghanistan Troops

Author: Adam Nagourney and Dalia Sussman

Source: *New York Times*, December 9, 2009, http://www.nytimes.com/2009/12/10/world/asia/10poll.html.

Read the following extract from the above article and answer the related questions.

> A bare majority of Americans support President Obama's plan to send 30,000 more troops to Afghanistan, but many are skeptical that the United States can count on Afghanistan as a partner in the fight or that the escalation would reduce the chances of a domestic terrorist attack, according to the latest *New York Times*/CBS News poll.
>
> ...
>
> The support for Mr. Obama's Afghanistan policy is decidedly ambivalent, and the nation's appetite for any intervention is limited. Over all, Americans support sending the troops in by 51% to 43%, while 55% said setting a date to begin troop withdrawals was a bad idea.
>
> ...
>
> The poll was conducted by telephone from Friday through Tuesday night, with 1,031 respondents, and has a margin of sampling error of plus or minus three percentage points.

Questions

1. About how many people in the sample supported sending more troops to Afghanistan?

2. Suppose the headline had read as follows: "Poll Finds Slim Majority of All Americans Back More Afghanistan Troops." What is wrong with the use of the word "majority" in the previous sentence?

BEYOND THE NUMBERS 4.5

ME in Practice

Name: ______________________________ Section Number: ________

To be graded, all assignments must be completed and submitted on the original book page.

EXHIBIT 1

Is It Warm in Here?

Title: Americans Do Care About Climate Change

Author: Annie Leonard

Source: *New York Times* May 8, 2014, http://www.nytimes.com/roomfordebate/2014/05/08/climate-debate-isnt-so-heated-in-the-us/americans-do-care-about-climate-change.

The following is an excerpt from the *New York Times* article:

> Americans do care about climate change. Polls showing lower levels of concern than in some countries don't tell the whole story. I travel widely around the U.S., attending meetings at schools, churches and community gatherings. Everywhere I go, I see people who are not only concerned about climate change, but are actively working on solutions.
>
> Nearly two-thirds (67%) of Americans accept the scientific evidence of global warming; fewer than one in six remain in denial. Two-thirds of Americans, including a majority of Republicans, want stricter limits on air pollution from power plants.

The full report referenced by Leonard's article tells us that the original survey was conducted by the Pew Research Center in October 2013. There was a (95%) margin of sampling error of about 2.9% associated with the entire sample.

Questions

1. What are the Pew Center poll's sample and statistic?

2. What are the population and the parameter?

3. Using the ME given in the article, construct a confidence interval for the true proportion of all Americans who accept the scientific evidence of global warming.

4. When the data were broken down into subgroups, such as Republicans and Democrats, the associated MEs increased. Explain why that makes sense.

5. Polls often select something equivalent to an SRS (for example, likely voters) and then break that selection down into smaller subgroups, (for example, men and women). Margins of error are then computed for the smaller subgroups using the same formula as for the original sample, only with a different sample size. Argue that these smaller subgroups can be considered simple random samples.

BEYOND THE NUMBERS 4.6

Practicing What You Know

Name: ______________________________ Section Number: ________

To be graded, all assignments must be completed and submitted on the original book page.

Read *The Times* excerpt below. Then, answer the questions that follow.

Americans and Their Guns

Title: Poll: Majority of Americans Back Stricter Gun Laws

Authors: Sarah Dutton, Jennifer De Pinto, Anthony Salvanto, Fred Backus and Leigh Ann Caldwell

Source: *CBS News* January 17, 2013, http://www.cbsnews.com/8301-250_162-57564597/poll-majority-of-americans-back-stricter-gun-laws/.

As the president outlined sweeping new proposals aimed to reduce gun violence, a new *CBS News/New York Times* poll found that Americans back the central components of the president's proposals, including background checks, a national gun sale database, limits on high capacity magazines and a ban on semi-automatic weapons. Asked if they generally back stricter gun laws, more than half of respondents—54%—support stricter gun laws ... That is a jump from April—before the Newtown and Aurora shootings—when only 39% backed stricter gun laws but about the same as ten years ago.

...

This poll was conducted by telephone from January 11–15, 2013, among 1,110 adults nationwide. Phone numbers were dialed from samples of both standard land-line and cell phones. The error due to sampling for results based on the entire sample could be plus or minus three percentage points.

Questions

1. What are the sample and the statistic for the *CBS News* poll?

2. What are the population and the parameter?

3. This survey reports a margin of sampling error of about 3%. Follow your instructor's instructions to confirm the margin of error.

4. Find an 80% confidence interval for the true proportion of Americans who "generally back stricter gun laws." What percent decrease in width is this interval from a 95% interval?

5. The headline on this article refers to the "Majority of Americans." Carefully explain if the reference is to the population or the sample. Is the headline statistically defensible? Be sure to offer a clear defense of your answer by citing appropriate statistical evidence from the article.

BEYOND THE NUMBERS 4.7

The Empirical Rule

Name: Laney Ratterman Section Number: 009

To be graded, all assignments must be completed and submitted on the original book page.

Background

A bell-shaped distribution is characterized by where it peaks (mean) and how spread out it is (standard deviation). We already know that a bell-shaped sampling distribution is important to the construction of a margin of error and the associated confidence interval. However, bell-shaped distributions also contain useful probabilistic information about the variable being described. The following well-known rule addresses this connection.

Empirical Rule:

Suppose a bell-shaped distribution has a mean μ and a standard deviation σ. Then:

a. About 68% of all observations represented by that distribution will fall within one standard deviation of the mean.

b. About 95% will fall within two standard deviations of the mean.

c. About 99.7% will fall within three standard deviations of the mean.

Graphically:

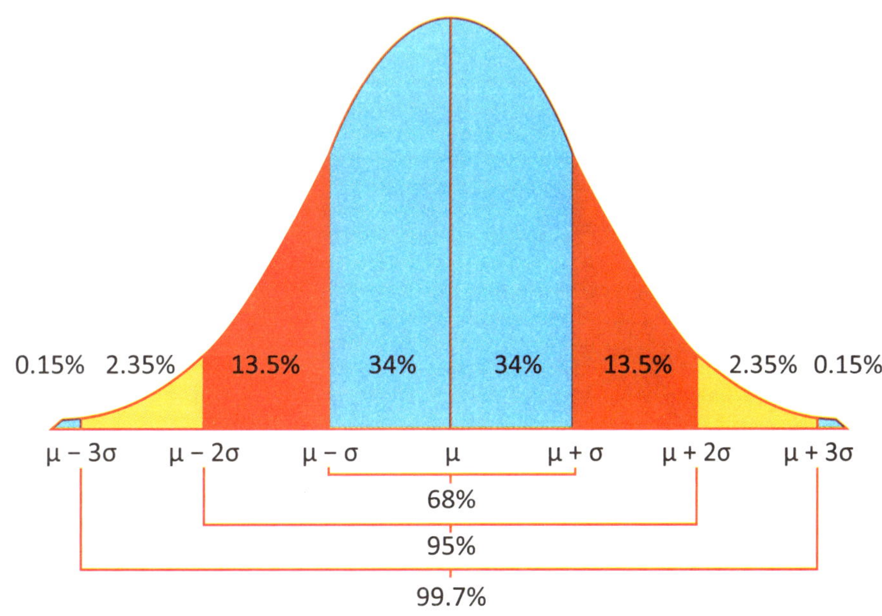

EXHIBIT 1

Face in Class Book

In a 2012 *Washington Post* article entitled "Is College Too Easy? As Study Time Falls, Debate Rises," Daniel de Vise reports that "over the past half-century, the [average] amount of time college students actually study—read, write and otherwise prepare for class—has dwindled from 24 hours a week to about 15 ...." No standard deviation is given, but let's assume that standard deviation is 2.5 hours.

Questions

1. Suppose a college student is selected at random. Use the empirical rule to estimate how likely it is that this student studies between 10 and 17.5 hours per week.

   81.5%

2. Suppose a college student is selected at random. Use the empirical rule to estimate how likely it is that this student studies between 17.5 and 20 hours per week.

   13.5%

3. Suppose a college student is selected at random. Use the empirical rule to estimate how likely it is that this student studies more than 20 hours per week.

   2.5%

4. Estimate the average number of hours you study each week. How many standard deviations away from the mean do you fall?

   x = # of hours you study every week

   $$\frac{x - 15}{2.5}$$

EXHIBIT 2

Class on Facebook

A 2012[1] study measured "the efficacy of social networking systems as instructional tools." The study surveyed 186 students about the use of social networking systems as an active part of the semester class structure. One question asked and answered by 181 of the 186 students, along with the results received, is shown below.

Question from the study: There are no specific benefits that make Facebook a better forum for class discussions and announcements than a learning management system like Blackboard. Do you agree or disagree?

TABLE 4.3 Survey Results

Response	Number of Subjects Choosing This Response
1 – Strongly Disagree	9
2 – Disagree	43
3 – Neutral/Undecided	59
4 – Agree	52
5 – Strongly Agree	18

Make sure you can read the table. If you are having trouble interpreting the data, ask your instructor to explain it. The mean of these 181 answers is 3.15 and the standard deviation is 1.05.

Questions

1. Use the empirical rule to estimate how likely it is that an answer to this question will be in the interval 2.10 to 4.20. What was the actual percentage of answers in this interval?

   0.683 → empirical

   61.33 → actual

2. Use the empirical rule to estimate how likely it is that an answer to this question will be above 4.20. What was the actual percentage of answers in this interval?

   0.159 → empirical

   0.994 → actual

[1] Buzzetto-More, N. "Social Networking in Undergraduate Education," *Interdisciplinary Journal of Information, Knowledge, and Management* Volume 7, 2012.

3. This example is somewhat atypical since only five outcomes are possible and the empirical rule doesn't strictly apply. It still provides useful estimates, however. Graph the distribution of these 181 answers and show that it is, indeed, bell-shaped. Use computer software (such as StatKey, Microsoft Excel, or Apple Numbers) to create this plot. Cut and paste the plot (literally or electronically, depending on how you are instructed to turn this exercise in) in the space below.

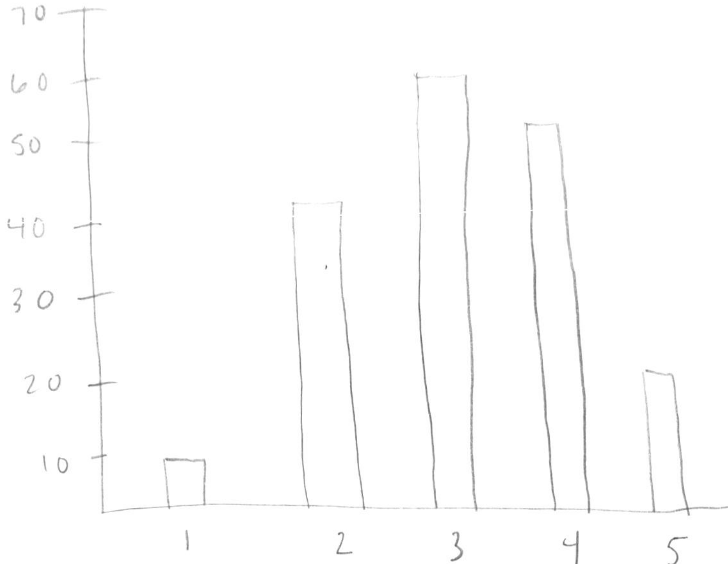

4. Confirm that the mean is 3.15 and the standard deviation is 1.05, as claimed. Use computer software (such as StatKey, Microsoft Excel, or Apple Numbers) to do this. Provide detailed instructions as to how you accomplished this task.

BEYOND THE NUMBERS 4.8

Confidence Intervals for Means

Name: ______________________________ Section Number: ________

To be graded, all assignments must be completed and submitted on the original book page.

EXHIBIT 1

Inaugural Intervals

A random sample of 10 U.S. presidents was taken and the age at inauguration recorded. See the table on the right.

TABLE 4.4 Inaugural Intervals

President	Age at Inauguration
James Madison	57 years, 353 days
Martin Van Buren	54 years, 89 days
Millard Fillmore	50 years, 183 days
Warren G. Harding	55 years, 122 days
William McKinley	54 years, 34 days
William Howard Taft	51 years, 170 days
George Washington	57 years, 67 days
Benjamin Harrison	55 years, 196 days
Franklin D. Roosevelt	51 years, 33 days
Ulysses S. Grant	46 years, 311 days

Questions

1. Find the sample mean of these 10 presidents' ages in days at the time of their inauguration. You are required to use a software package (such as StatKey, Microsoft Excel, or Apple Numbers) as directed by your instructor.

2. Find the sample standard deviation of these 10 presidents' ages in days. You are required to use a software package (such as StatKey, Microsoft Excel, or Apple Numbers) as directed by your instructor.

3. What is t^* for a 90% confidence interval?

4. Compute a 90% confidence interval for the true average age (in days) of all U.S. presidents, up to and including President Trump, at the time of inauguration.

5. Carefully interpret the interval you computed in Question 4.

6. Do some research on your own and determine the true average age of *all* 45 U.S. presidents, up to and including President Trump. You are required to use a software package (such as StatKey, Microsoft Excel, or Apple Numbers) as directed by your instructor. See if the interval you computed in Question 4 contains this true average. Whether it does or doesn't, explain the chances of that outcome happening.

THEME 5

Hypothesis Testing

BEYOND THE NUMBERS 5.1

Treatment Decision: Effective or Not?

Name: Laney Ratterman Section Number: [illegible]

To be graded, all assignments must be completed and submitted on the original book page.

EXHIBIT 1

Pumpkin Powered Prostates

Pumpkins and Prostate Health

Title: Pumpkin Seed Oil May Be a Halloween Treat

Author: Elena Conis

Source: *Los Angeles Times*, October 25, 2010, http://articles.latimes.com/2010/oct/25/health/la-he-nutrition-lab-pumpkin-20101025

In the News ...

According to the article in the *Los Angeles Times* by Elena Conis, for centuries pumpkin seeds have been a home remedy used to control or increase the frequency of urination in adults, children, and livestock. Knowing this about pumpkin seeds has prompted researchers to explore the possibility of a link between eating the seeds and better prostate health.

German researchers have been very involved in exploring this possible connection. The article summarized one study, the results of which were published in a German journal in 2000. According to the *Los Angeles Times*, the study:

> randomly selected among about 500 men to take either 1,000 milligrams of pumpkin seed oil extract or a placebo every day for 12 months. Symptoms improved in 65% of the men who took the oil, which the researchers interpreted as a promising (and statistically significant) result, even though symptoms also improved in 54% of the men who took the placebo.

Questions

1. Define the parameters of interest and state the null and alternative hypothesis.

parameter: proportion of people [illegible]

H_0: [illegible] $= P_p$

H_a: [illegible] $> P_p$

2. Should the null be rejected? Why or why not?

Yes, there was not a big difference between men who took the oil and [illegible] → result was statistically significant

EXHIBIT 2

Stutter Stopper?

Drugs for Stutterers

Title: Drug for Stutterers Shows Promise: Indevus Says Pill Reduced Incidents for Most in 1st Trial

Author: Stephen Heuser

Source: *Boston Globe,* May 25, 2006, http://www.boston.com/yourlife/health/diseases/articles/2006/05/25/drug_for_stutterers_shows_promise/

The following is an extract from a *Boston Globe* article on stuttering:

> A potential pill to treat stuttering took a step forward yesterday when Indevus Pharmaceuticals Inc. of Lexington said its experimental drug reduced stuttering in a majority of patients in its first clinical trial.
>
> The 132-patient trial is the largest human test ever conducted on a drug for stuttering, according to the company.
>
> ...
>
> The Indevus drug, called pagoclone, was given to 88 patients in escalating doses, with the rest of the trial subjects receiving a placebo. The patients were then tracked using several widely accepted measures of stuttering.
>
> ...
>
> On a third rating scale, based on doctors' impressions, the pagoclone patients scored a "numerically superior rating" to the placebo group, but the finding did not reach statistical significance.

Questions

1. Define the parameters of interest and state the null and alternative hypothesis

2. Should the null be rejected? Why or why not?

BEYOND THE NUMBERS 5.2

Statistical Significance in the Media—Part I

Name: Laney Ratterman Section Number: 009

To be graded, all assignments must be completed and submitted on the original book page.

EXHIBIT 1

Prescription to Pass

Drug Safety

Title: Trial Intensifies Concerns about Safety of Vytorin

Author: Alex Berenson

Source: *New York Times,* July 22, 2008, http://www.nytimes.com/2008/07/22/business/22drug.html

The following is an extract from a *New York Times* article on Vytorin:

> In a clinical trial, the cholesterol-lowering drug Vytorin did not help people with heart-valve disease avoid further heart problems but did appear to increase their risk of cancer, scientists reported Monday.
>
> ...
>
> Vytorin and Zetia, a companion drug, are prescribed each month to almost three million people worldwide and are among the world's top-selling medicines.
>
> ...
>
> In the Seas trial, which involved nearly 1,900 patients whose heart valves were partially blocked, participants were given either Vytorin or a placebo pill that contained no medicine. Scientists hoped that the trial would show that patients taking Vytorin would have a lower risk of needing valve replacement surgery or having heart failure. But the drug did not show those benefits.
>
> "No significant difference was observed between the treatment groups for the combined primary endpoint," Dr. Terje Pedersen, the principal investigator for the study and a professor medicine at Ulleval University Hospital in Norway, said. The primary endpoint is the result that scientists hope to prove when they conduct a clinical trial.
>
> However, patients taking Vytorin in the Seas trial did have a sharply higher risk of developing and dying from cancer. In the trial 102 patients taking Vytorin developed cancer, compared with 67 taking the placebo. Of those, 39 people taking Vytorin died from their cancer, compared with 23 taking placebo.
>
> The absolute numbers of cancer cases were relatively small. But they reached statistical significance, meaning the odds were less than 5% that they were the result of chance.

Question

1. When the phrase "significant difference" is used, define the parameters of interest and state the null and alternative hypothesis.

parameter: difference of proportions in those who developed/died from cancer

$H_0 = P_1 = P_2$

$H_a = P_1 < P_2$

2. When the phrase "significant difference" is used, should the null be rejected? Why or why not?

The null should be rejected because there is not enough evidence to conclude.

3. When the phrase "statistical significance" is used, define the parameters of interest and state the null and alternative hypothesis.

parameter: proportion of those who got/developed cancer

$H_0 = P_1 = P_2$

$H_a = P_1 > P_2$

4. When the phrase "statistical significance" is used, should the null be rejected? Why or why not?

The null should. be rejected when the phrase statistical significance is used.

BEYOND THE NUMBERS 5.3

Statistical Significance in the Media—Part II

Name: Laney Ratterman Section Number: 009

To be graded, all assignments must be completed and submitted on the original book page.

EXHIBIT 1

Should I Eat My Vegetables?

Eat Your Veggies

Title: Eating Vegetables Doesn't Stop Cancer

Author: Tara Parker-Pope

Source: *New York Times,* April 8, 2010, http://well.blogs.nytimes.com/2010/04/08/eating-vegetables-doesnt-stop-cancer/

A recent *New York Times* article reported, "A major study tracking the eating habits of 478,000 Europeans suggests that consuming lots of fruits and vegetables has little if any effect on preventing cancer." The study, which was published in *The Journal of the National Cancer Institute*, "tracked 142,605 men and 335,873 women for an average of nearly nine years. Eating more vegetables was associated with a small but statistically significant reduction in cancer risk."

Questions

1. What was the conclusion in their test? Did they reject H_0 or fail to reject H_0? How do you know?

They concluded that eating more vegetables was associated w/ a small but statistically significant reduction in cancer risk. They rejected H_0 because their result was statistically significant.

2. What do we know about the *p*-value compared to alpha?

p-value is less than alpha

3. Which error could we be making (Type I or Type II)?

Type 1 error

4. What does this article tell you about statistical and practical significance?

This result, while statistically significant, is not [illegible] the risk of getting cancer.

BEYOND THE NUMBERS 5.4

Statistical Significance in the Media—Part III

Name: Lorey Patterman Section Number: 009

To be graded, all assignments must be completed and submitted on the original book page.

EXHIBIT 1

Dangerous Training?

Crash Test

Title: Motorcycle Training Does Not Reduce Crash Risk, Study Says

Author: Cheryl Jensen

Source: *New York Times,* April 5, 2010, http://wheels.blogs.nytimes.com/2010/04/05/motorcycle-training-does-not-reduce-crash-risk-study-says/

Consider the following statements from a recent *New York Times* article discussing a recent study by the Highway Loss Data Institute regarding the effectiveness of training courses in improving motorcycle safety, and consider the questions below. The article says:

> What is not so certain are the safety benefits of mandatory training programs for young drivers in some states. The study compared insurance claims in four states that require riders under 21 to take courses with states that do not. The study noted a 10% increase in crashes in states that required the courses."
>
> But that finding wasn't "statistically significant," Ms. McCartt [senior vice president for research at the Insurance Institute] said. That means the increase might or might not be real, although the institute found it worth noting. "It is important that it was going in the opposite direction of what people would expect," she said.

Questions

1. Define the parameters of interest and state the null and alternative hypothesis.

parameter: young motorcycle drivers μ_1: true avg crashes (w/ courses)

$H_0: \mu_1 = \mu_2$ $H_a: \mu_1 > \mu_2$ μ_2: true avg crashes (w/out courses)

2. What do we know about the *p*-value compared to alpha? Which Type of error could we be making?

The p-value is larger than alpha and we could be making a type II error.

EXHIBIT 2

Vouching for Vouchers

Voucher Controversy

Title: White House Ignores Evidence of How D.C. School Vouchers Work

Author: Editorial Board Opinion

Source: *Washington Post,* March 29, 2011, http://www.washingtonpost.com/opinions/white-house-ignores-evidence-of-how-dc-school-vouchers-work/2011/03/29/AFFsnHyB_story.html

Consider the following statements from a recent *Washington Post* editorial discussing the Obama strongly worded dismissal of school vouchers. The article says:

> That dismissal might come as a surprise to Patrick J. Wolf, the principal investigator who helped conduct the rigorous studies of the D.C. Opportunity Scholarship Program and who has more than a decade of experience evaluating school choice programs.
>
> Here's what Mr. Wolf had to say about the program in Feb. 16 testimony to the Senate Committee on Homeland Security and Governmental Operations. "In my opinion, by demonstrating statistically significant experimental impacts on boosting high school graduation rates and generating a wealth of evidence suggesting that students also benefited in reading achievement, the DC OSP has accomplished what few educational interventions can claim: It markedly improved important education outcomes for low-income inner-city students."

Questions

1. The phrase "statistically significant" is used in Mr. Wolf's testimony. Define the parameters of interest and state the null and alternative hypothesis.

parameter: P_1 grad rate (in OSP system)
P_2: grad rate (not in OSP system)

$H_0: P_1 = P_2$

$H_a: P_1 > P_2$

2. What do we know about the *p*-value compared to alpha? Which Type of error could we be making?

The p-value is smaller than alpha which means we could be making a Type I error.

BEYOND THE NUMBERS 5.5

Practical Significance versus Statistical Significance

Name: Laney Ratterman Section Number: 009

To be graded, all assignments must be completed and submitted on the original book page.

EXHIBIT 1

Effect Size Matters

From *Time* Health

Women in the flibanserin group self-reported an average of 2.8 sexually satisfying events in the four-week baseline period. In the final four weeks of the 24-week study period, those women reported an average of 4.5 sexually satisfying events, a more than 50% increase. Women in the placebo group reported an average increase from 2.7 events to 3.7. The difference in effect between flibanserin and the placebo—about 0.8 sexually satisfying events—was statistically significant, the drug company said. The side effects from the drug, which included dizziness and fatigue, among others, were mild to moderate and transient.

Read more: http://www.time.com/time/health/article/0,8599,1939884,00.html

Questions

1. Explain where the "about 0.8 sexually satisfying events" statement comes from.

This statement comes from the placebo group

2. Read the description of the study carefully. What was the difference in effect between flibanserin and the placebo on an average weekly basis? Was the difference impressively large? Explain.

The flibanserin group had a 50% increase while the placebo group had an increase of 0.8. The difference wasn't impressively large, but it was statistically significant.

$\frac{0.8}{4} = 0.2$ events/week

EXHIBIT 2

Catching a Breath

Stopping Sleep Apnea

Title: Statistical versus Clinical Significance: They Are Not the Same

Author: The Skeptical Scalpel

Source: *Skeptical Scalpel,* August 8, 2011, http://skepticalscalpel.blogspot.com/2011/08/statistical-vs-clinical-significance.html

In reference to an article that appeared on MedPage Today, August 5th, 2011 ("Compression Stocking Help Sleep Apnea," by Michael Smith), the Skeptical Scalpel writes:

> MedPage Today featured an article about the beneficial effects of daytime wearing of compression stockings on obstructive sleep apnea. The premise was that increased edema in the neck could be caused by fluid coming from the legs when patients were in the supine position at night. Twelve patients who served as their own controls wore compression stockings for a week and then no stockings for a week alternating. The stockings lowered the amount of fluid in the neck by 60%, a statistically significant difference. So far, so good.
>
> This resulted in another highly statistically significant finding, which was a 36% reduction in episodes of apnea [cessation of breathing] and hypopnea [inadequate breathing]. Sounds good, right? The problem is that the average number of episodes of apnea/hypopnea decreased from 48 per hour to 31 per hour. Patients experiencing more than 30 episodes of apnea/hypopnea per hour are classified as having severe obstructive sleep apnea. This means that the treatment only put the patients in the low range of severe obstructive sleep apnea. They still would require maximum therapy. Is a reduction in apnea/hypopnea episodes that does not move the patient out of the severe category really clinically significant? It does not seem so to me.

Questions

1. Define the parameters of interest and state the null and alternative hypothesis.

μ_1 people who wore neck compression μ_2: People who didn't wear neck compression

$H_0: \mu_1 = \mu_2$ $H_a: \mu_1 < \mu_2$

2. The Skeptical Scalpel is making a point about practical significance. What is that point? Do you agree? Even though the result is statistically significant, it is not practically significant because the patients were still in the range of having severe sleep apnea. I agree with their point of view.

BEYOND THE NUMBERS 5.6

A Practical Discussion

Name: Laney Ratterman Section Number: 009

To be graded, all assignments must be completed and submitted on the original book page.

EXHIBIT 1

The N Crowd

An MD/Ph.D at a major research institution is studying a new cannabis-based pain medication. The patients who volunteer for the study are randomly divided into two groups. Group 1 is given a placebo (Treatment 1). After one hour, group members rate the effectiveness of the pain relief on a scale of 1 to 100. Group 2 is given the new drug (Treatment 2), then group members rate the pain relief effectiveness in a similar way. Initially, only 25 volunteers were available for each group. By the end of the month, however, there were 25,000 volunteers in each group, making this the largest clinical trial in recent memory. Amazingly, there is only a one-point difference between the ratings of the placebo group and the ratings of the active treatment group at each stage. Formally, the following choice has to be made:

- H_0: Treatment 2 is no different than Treatment 1
- H_A: Treatment 2 is more effective than Treatment 1

Questions

1. For the second, third, and fourth weeks, determine the *p*-value and state if the test has a statistically significant result. Use significance level α = 0.05.

TABLE 5.1 Statistically Significant Results

	1st Week	2nd Week	3rd Week	4th Week
Sample size in each group (N)	25	250	2,500	25,000
Standard deviation in each group	20	20	20	20
Treatment 1 mean (placebo)	50	50	50	50
Treatment 2 mean (new drug)	51	51	51	51
p-value	0.430	0.288	0.039	0.000
Statistically significant? Check 'Yes' or 'No'	☐ Yes ☑ No	☐ Yes ☐ No	☐ Yes ☐ No	☐ Yes ☐ No

2. What does this exercise have to say about the relationship between sample size and statistical significance? Be very specific in your answer.

The larger the sample size, the more likely you are to get statistically significant results.

3. What does this exercise have to say about whether one can reliably infer practical significance from statistical significance? This exercise shows that you cannot reliably infer practical significance from statistical significance because the p-value changes drastically from the first to the last trial

4. Do you think a study's sample size can ever be too large? Explain your reasoning.

Yes, if a sample is larger, it allows for more accurate results by testing a larger number of people in a population. It can lead to confusion between practical and statistical significance when the true effect is too small to care about.

BEYOND THE NUMBERS 5.7

Origins of Power

Name: Laney Ratterman Section Number: ________

To be graded, all assignments must be completed and submitted on the original book page.

Background

In hypothesis testing, the Type II error rate is the empirical probability of failing to reject H_0 when you should. This rate is typically denoted by the Greek letter β. The power of the hypothesis test is 1-β. Think of it as the probability of choosing H_A when H_A is the right choice.

The computation of power can be a complex endeavor, even for elementary forms of H_0 and H_A. However, we can gain valuable insights into the power of a statistical test by using a freely-available online tool to handle all of the complex computations for us.

EXHIBIT 1

Power and Beauty

Title: Power and Sample Size.com

Author: HyLown Consulting, LLC

Source: http://powerandsamplesize.com/Calculators/Test-1-Mean/1-Sample-Equality

Suppose you are interested in how people rate their looks on a 20 point scale, with a score of 0 meaning *unbearably ugly* and a score of 20 meaning *hopelessly gorgeous*. Later in this workbook, you will learn how to test the following hypothesis mathematically:

- H_0: true population average is 10
- H_A: true population average is not 10

What we want to do is to answer the question:

"How likely is it that we will fail to reject H_0 if H_0 is truly false?"

The answer to this question leads us to the Type II error rate, from which power is easily computed. To come up with an answer, we first have to ask:

"What is the true average if H_0 is false?"

H_A only tells us, in this case, that the true average is something other than 10. We will begin by considering four possible averages that are different from 10: 10.5, 11, 11.5, and 12.

Questions

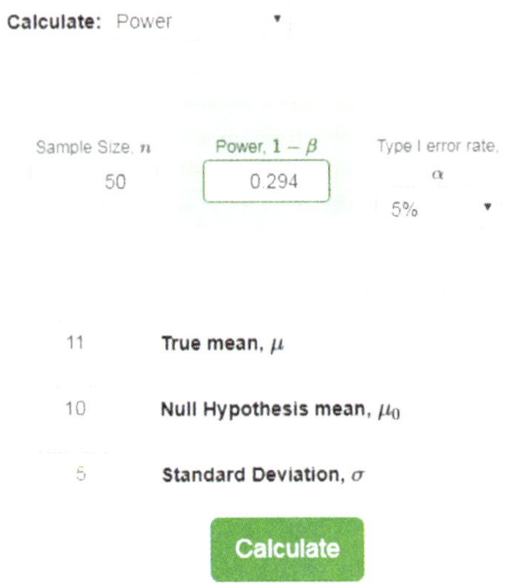

1. Access the applet at the web address listed in the Source line above. When the applet page loads:
   - Select "Power"
   - Enter the sample size (e.g. 50)
   - Enter True Mean (e.g. 11)
   - Enter Hypothesized Mean (always 10 for this problem)
   - Enter the Standard Deviation as 5
   - Leave the alpha level (Type I error rate) fixed at 5%
   - Hit Calculate
   - Record the Power value

   Do this for all True Mean and Sample Size combinations shown in the table below. One row is already done for you. Make sure you can confirm those entries and then finish finding the rest of the entries in the table. It is safest to reload the page between each calculation.

TABLE 5.2 Power Value Results

Power Table	Possible Real Values of the Population Average			
Sample Size	**10.5**	**11**	**11.5**	**12**
10	0.0619	0.0974	0.1584	0.245
50	0.1095	**0.29**	0.5652	0.[illegible]082
100	0.1708	0.5171	0.8515	0.9795
1,000	0.8859	1	1	1
10,000	1	1	1	1

2. Look at the table. How does power change as sample size changes, regardless of the true average?

   The power level gets closer to 1 as the sample size gets larger.

3. Look at the table. How does power change as the possible true average changes, regardless of sample size? The power level increases as the true average increases regardless of sample size

   power = 1 - β

4. What would happen to power if you changed alpha? Investigate that question using the online calculator that you used to fill out the table above.

   If you changed α from 5% to 10% then the power would get larger. If you changed α from 5% to 2.5%, then power would get smaller.

BEYOND THE NUMBERS 5.8

Computations versus Understanding

Name: Laney Katterman Section Number: 009

To be graded, all assignments must be completed and submitted on the original book page.

Introduction

It is important that you be able to compute correctly. However, computation prowess is no substitute for a deeper understanding of what you are doing and why. This is especially true in the field of statistical science. At the undergraduate level, computations are pretty easy. At all levels, however, the underlying concepts are challenging. The following activity will demonstrate and elucidate this divide.

EXHIBIT 1

Eureka or Not?

Suppose that twenty identical experiments are taking place simultaneously around the world. The researchers are all studying the same drug, which they hope will improve the survival rate of the black-winged peckerwood finch after it has been infected with a particular type of tree mold. The survival rate left untreated is unfortunately only 32%. None of the researchers know about the others' work. The table to the right shows the results from the 20 different studies. In all cases, the significance level was α = 0.05 and the hypothesis being tested was the following:

$$H_0: p = 0.32$$

$$H_A: p > 0.32$$

TABLE 5.3 Finch Survival Rates

Site	Observed Survival Rate with Drug	Number of Finches Studied	Able to Reject H_0: $p = 0.32$?
1	0.35	$n = 100$	No
2	0.34	$n = 100$	No
3	0.31	$n = 100$	No
4	0.33	$n = 100$	No
5	0.33	$n = 100$	No
6	0.35	$n = 100$	No
7	0.35	$n = 100$	No
8	0.33	$n = 100$	No
9	0.30	$n = 100$	No
10	0.34	$n = 100$	No
11	0.34	$n = 100$	No
12	0.30	$n = 100$	No
13	0.34	$n = 100$	No
14	0.31	$n = 100$	No
15	0.31	$n = 100$	No
16	0.31	$n = 100$	No
17*	**0.45**	**$n = 100$**	**Yes**
18	0.30	$n = 100$	No
19	0.35	$n = 100$	No
20	0.33	$n = 100$	No

Questions

1. Use the data from Site 17 to confirm that the null could be rejected. What is the p-value associated with the result?

   p-value : 0.003 which is less than α : 0.05

2. Combine all of the studies ($n = 100 \times 20 = 2{,}000$) and test the hypothesis again. Confirm that it cannot be rejected. Report the overall observed survival rate and the p-value associated with the overall test.

   count : 667

   sample : 2000

   p-value $\geq \alpha = 0.05$

3. We have a dilemma. Nineteen of the sites don't seek publication because their results are not significant. Site 17 gets published because the results produced there, with an identical experiment, are significant. We know (though the researchers don't) that if we combine the results from all 20 sites, we will not be able to support the alternative. Describe what it means to have a significance level of $\alpha = 0.05$, and explain what has likely happened here in light of that definition.

   α 0.05 means a Type I error rate 1 test out of 20 made a Type I error.

4. Do you think a ground-breaking scientific study should be replicated before it can be published? Why or why not? What steps should the scientific community take to improve study validity?

   Yes [illegible] guard against type I errors. [illegible] setting of a [illegible] hypothesis.

BEYOND THE NUMBERS 5.9

Role of Sample Size

Name: Laney Katterman Section Number: ________

To be graded, all assignments must be completed and submitted on the original book page.

EXHIBIT 1

Better than Chance?

You have spent a great deal of time so far testing hypotheses involving proportions. Let's focus on the one-tailed version for the moment.

$$H_0: p = p_0$$

$$H_A: p > p_0$$

Suppose that you are developing a new pill designed to help students guess better on yes/no test questions. If students guess totally at random, they have a 50–50 chance of getting it right. You want to show that students perform better after taking your pill so that you can get create some interest in crowd-based funding for production and marketing costs. Unfortunately, when testing the pill's effectiveness, you always ended up with 51% of the treatment group getting their yes/no questions correct.

Questions

1. Consider the following hypothesis. Complete the entries in the table below for the different sample sizes shown. Remember that $\hat{p}$ is 0.51 in all cases.

$$H_0: p = 0.50$$

$$H_A: p > 0.50$$

TABLE 5.4 Hypothesis Results

Sample Size	One-Tailed *p*-Value	Statistically Significant Results? (yes or no)
100	0.448 0.464	no
1,000	0.293 0.266	no
10,000	0.025 0.025	yes
100,000	0.000 0.000	yes

2. Look at the table. What happens to the *p*-value as the sample size increases?

The p-value gets smaller as the sample size increases

3. After you ran enough people through your study, you were able to report that your results were statistically significant and that you would begin seeking funding. Give and defend two reasons why you are still likely to have an unconvincing case.

• Only 1% increase from 50% isn't practically significant

• getting [illegible] people in order to make it statistically significant isn't very practical

EXHIBIT 2

Crowd Control

Title: Duration of Sleep Contributes to Next-Day Pain Report in the General Population

Author: R. Edwards, et al.

Source: *Pain 137* (2008) 202–207.

The authors of this study interviewed participants from the general population. These participants recorded both the number of hours they slept during the previous sleep period and the frequency of their pain symptoms. Pain was recorded on a five-point scale. A summary of the resulting data is presented in the table below:

Question

1. A comparison of patients in the 0–3 hour category to those in the 11+ hour category is not statistically significant, despite a difference in means of 0.42. However, a comparison of patients in the 5-hour category to those in the 8-hour category *is* statistically significant, even though the difference in means is only 0.19. Give a solid reason as to why you think this is so. What practical implication does this have for our understanding of testing results?

The sample size [illegible] which makes it easier to see statistically significant results

TABLE 5.5 Pain Relief Results

Sleep (Hours)	Average Pain Rating	Standard Deviation	Sample Size
0–3	1.36	1.51	75
4	1.13	1.36	166
5	0.94	1.29	434
6	0.79	1.11	1,138
7	0.73	1.11	1,568
8	0.75	1.13	1,557
9	0.71	1.09	339
10	1.24	1.4	119
11+	1.78	1.59	66

BEYOND THE NUMBERS 5.10

Practice with Proportions

Name: Laney Ratterman Section Number: 009

To be graded, all assignments must be completed and submitted on the original book page.

Questions

1. The CEO of a large electric utility claims that more than 80% of his customers are very satisfied with the service they receive. To test this claim, the local newspaper surveyed 100 customers using simple random sampling. Among the sampled customers, 81% said that they were very satisfied. Do these results provide sufficient evidence to accept or reject the CEO's claim? To answer this question, you will have to test the hypothesis H_0: $p = 0.80$ versus H_A $p > 0.80$. Assume a significance level of $\alpha = 0.05$. Report a *p*-value, say whether you reject or fail to reject H_0, and explain why you made the choice you did.

$H_0 = p = 0.8$

$H_A = p > 0.8$

$SE = \sqrt{\frac{p(1-p)}{n}} = \sqrt{\frac{0.8(0.2)}{100}}$

$z = \frac{\hat{p} - p_0}{SE} = \frac{0.81 - 0.8}{0.04} = \frac{0.01}{0.04} = 0.25$

p-value : 0.401

do not reject H_0
no evidence of H_A

2. Patients with advanced cancers of the stomach, bronchus, colon, ovary, and breast were treated with ascorbate. Their survival time post-diagnosis was then monitored.[1] The resulting data set is available at statconcepts.com/student-resources/sta-296-datasets or in the appendix. Test the hypothesis that the proportion of cancer patients treated with ascorbate who will survive more than a year is larger than 0.40. Assume a significance level of $\alpha = 0.05$. Report a *p*-value, say whether you reject or fail to reject H_0, and explain why you made the choice you did.

· the data has sample size n=63, count survival is 27

$\hat{p} = \frac{27}{63} \approx 0.42857$

$H_0 = p = 0.40$

$H_a = p > 0.40$

null value $p_0 = 0.4$

$z = \frac{\hat{p} - p_0}{SE} = \frac{0.42857 - 0.4}{\sqrt{\frac{0.4(1-0.4)}{63}}} = 0.463$

statkey p-value = 0.322 > α = 0.05

[1] Cameron, E. and Pauling, L. (1978). Supplemental ascorbate in the supportive treatment of cancer: re evaluation of prolongation of survival times in terminal human cancer. Proceedings of the National Academy of Science USA, 75, 4538–4542.

3. Refer to the cancer data referenced in Question 2. Test the hypothesis that the proportion of breast cancer patients treated with ascorbate who will survive more than a year is larger than 0.75. Assume a significance level of α = 0.05. Report a *p*-value, say whether you reject or fail to reject H_0, and explain why you made the choice you did. Are you surprised by this outcome? Why or why not?

· sample size of breast cancer is $n = 10$

↳ count is 8 → $\hat{p} = 0.8$

$H_0: p = 0.75$

$H_a: p > 0.75$

$p_0 = 0.75$

· test statistic $z = \frac{0.8 - 0.75}{\sqrt{\frac{0.75(1-0.75)}{10}}} \approx 0.365$

statkey p-value = $0.358 > \alpha = 0.05$

do not reject Ho, no evidence of Ha

· we do not have evidence to conclude that more than 75% of breast cancer patients treated w/ ascorbate will survive more than a year

↳ I am not surprised by this outcome

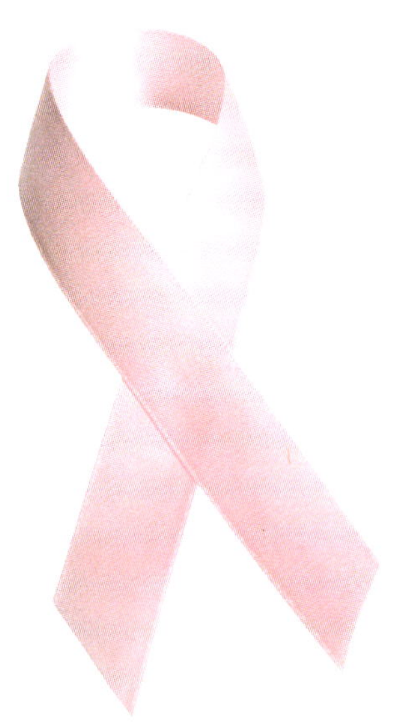

BEYOND THE NUMBERS 5.11

A Two-Sided Test

Name: Laney Patterman Section Number: ________

To be graded, all assignments must be completed and submitted on the original book page.

Please provide full solutions to the following problems.

1. Patients with advanced cancers of the stomach, bronchus, colon, ovary, and breast were treated with ascorbate. Their survival time post-diagnosis was then monitored.[1] The resulting data set is available at statconcepts.com/student-resources/sta-296-datasets or in the appendix. Test the hypothesis that the proportion of all cancer patients treated with ascorbate who will survive more than a year is different than 0.40. Assume a significance level of $\alpha = 0.05$. Report a *p*-value, say whether you reject or fail to reject H_0, and explain why you made the choice you did.

n = 63 count 27 → $\hat{p} = \frac{27}{63} = 0.42857$

$H_0 = p = 0.4$

$H_a = p > 0.4$

p-value = 0.322 × 2 = 0.644 > α = 0.05

do not reject Ho

no evidence of Ha

2. Suppose you want to test a hypothesis about a proportion, similar to what you've just done, but you don't know whether to use a two-sided or a one-sided test. You do know, however, that you have to have a Type I error rate of 0.05. You absent-mindedly take a look at your data results before forming H_A, and you notice $\hat{p} > p_0$. So you decide to go with a one-sided H_A. Why might this be considered cheating? Be very clear when explaining your reasons.

one-sided test has a p-value in half of that from a two sided test. A half is more likely to be less than α, and thus reject H_0 and conclude significance. Crossing a one-tailed or two tailed test should be decided before seeing the data. Generally, the two-tailed test is recommended for being conservative.

[1] Cameron, E. and Pauling, L. (1978). Supplemental ascorbate in the supportive treatment of cancer: re evaluation of prolongation of survival times in terminal human cancer. Proceedings of the National Academy of Science USA, 75, 4538–4542.

BEYOND THE NUMBERS 5.12

Single Mean Test

Name: Laney Ratterman Section Number: 009

To be graded, all assignments must be completed and submitted on the original book page.

Example

Drum Corps International sets field performance guidelines for all their competitive participants. Setup time, which occurs before a field performance, has to be practiced carefully in order to meet Drum Corps' time constraints. These time limits change from year to year, but the World Class division typically allots 3 minutes to set up, 2 minutes to do a pre-show, and then 12 minutes to perform the main show. Suppose Carolina Crown, the defending 2013 World Class division champions, has practiced the setup 30 times. They have achieved an average setup time of 3 minutes and 4 seconds with a standard deviation of 15.5 seconds. Test the hypothesis that the true mean time for setup is different than 3 minutes.

$$H_0: \mu = 180 \text{ secs}$$

$$H_A: \mu \neq 180 \text{ secs}$$

Questions

1. Crown's thirty hypothetical times are presented in the table to the right. Use the data to compute the *t*-test statistic and find the *p*-value.

$H_0 = \mu = 180$

$H_a = \mu \neq 180$

$\bar{X} = 184$

$s = 15.471$

p-value = 0.1674

$$\frac{\bar{X} - \mu_0}{\frac{s}{\sqrt{n}}} = \frac{184 - 180}{\frac{15.471}{\sqrt{30}}} = 1.416$$

2. Let's change the data some. Suppose the Attempt 23 time was erroneously recorded as 200 instead of 150. Re-test the hypothesis:

H_0: μ = 180 secs

H_A: μ ≠ 180 secs

Set the significance level as 0.10. Make sure you report what software you used, the two-tailed *p*-value, and your answer. Please note that depending on what software you use, you may have to compute the mean and standard deviation separately.

$\bar{X} = 185.67$

$s = 14.334$

$$t = \frac{185.67 - 180}{\frac{14.334}{\sqrt{30}}} = 2.1665$$

p-value = 0.03861

TABLE 5.6 Crown's Setup Times

Attempt	Setup Time
1	200
2	189
3	180
4	168
5	168
6	195
7	167
8	200
9	167
10	210
11	185
12	167
13	190
14	180
15	175
16	175
17	182
18	171
19	202
20	195
21	212
22	203
23	150
24	175
25	200
26	182
27	184
28	165
29	203
30	180

3. Reflect on your answer to Question 2. What can you say about how finicky this hypothesis test is given its reaction to a typo in one data point?

This hypothesis test is definitely very finicky since one typo in one data point can change a number by that much.

4. The Cadets Drum and Bugle Corps from Allentown, Pennsylvania, routinely compete with Carolina Crown in the World Class division. They are also subject to the same setup time restrictions. Suppose, based on 30 sample setups, that they have a sample mean of $\bar{x}$ = 184 seconds just like Crown. However, they have a standard deviation of just 5.1 seconds. Test the hypothesis shown. Use a significance level of 0.05. Make sure you report the two-tailed *p*-value and your answer. Explain the difference between the results you found for the Cadets and those for Crown.

H_0: μ = 180 secs

H_A: μ ≠ 180 secs

$\bar{x} = 184$ $\alpha = 0.05$

$s = 5.1$

$t = \frac{184 - 180}{\frac{5.1}{\sqrt{30}}} = 4.382$ p-value = 0.0001

↳ less than α

reject H_0

BEYOND THE NUMBERS 5.13

Confirming What We Read

Name: Laney Ratterman Section Number: 009

To be graded, all assignments must be completed and submitted on the original book page.

EXHIBIT 1

Mary Jane Brain

Title: Moderation of the Effect of Adolescent-Onset Cannabis Use on Adult Psychosis by a Functional Polymorphism in the Catechol-O-Methyltransferase Gene: Longitudinal Evidence of a Gene X Environment Interaction

Author: A. Caspi, et al.

Source: *Biol Psychiatry* 2005;57:1117–1127

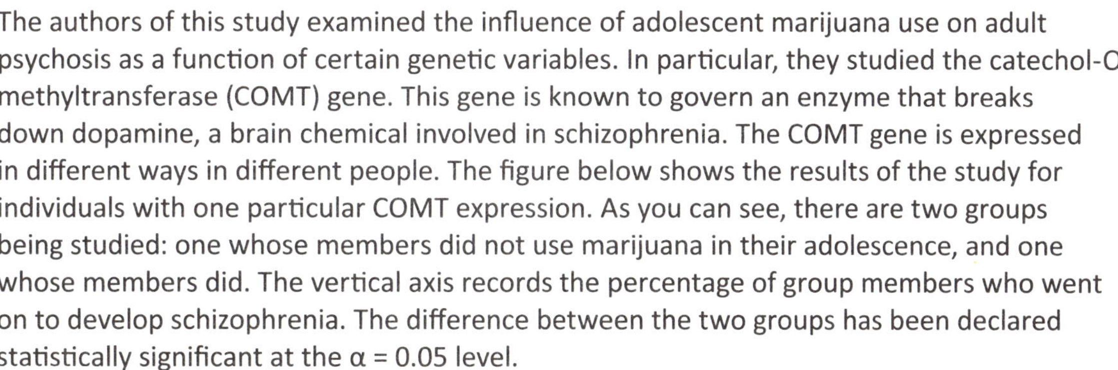

The authors of this study examined the influence of adolescent marijuana use on adult psychosis as a function of certain genetic variables. In particular, they studied the catechol-O methyltransferase (COMT) gene. This gene is known to govern an enzyme that breaks down dopamine, a brain chemical involved in schizophrenia. The COMT gene is expressed in different ways in different people. The figure below shows the results of the study for individuals with one particular COMT expression. As you can see, there are two groups being studied: one whose members did not use marijuana in their adolescence, and one whose members did. The vertical axis records the percentage of group members who went on to develop schizophrenia. The difference between the two groups has been declared statistically significant at the α = 0.05 level.

Question

1. Are the results statistically significant as claimed? Let the subscript 1 denote the "No Adolescent Marijuana Use" group, and let the subscript 2 denote the "Adolescent Marijuana Use" group." Test the hypotheses stated below:

$$H_0: p_1 = p_2$$

$$H_A: p_1 < p_2$$

$\hat{p}_1 = 0.023$ $\hat{p}_2 = 0.055$

normal approx. is not satisfied b/c $n_1\hat{p}_1 < 10$ and $n_2\hat{p}_2 < 10$.

Randomization test for diff in proportions

↳ left tail

p-value = 0.115 > α

↳ results are not significant

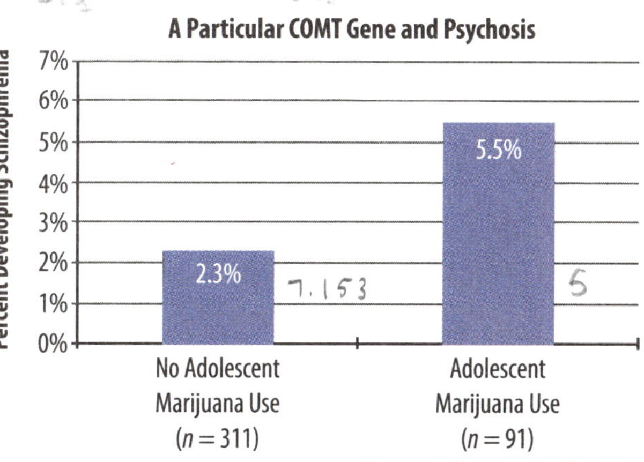

BEYOND THE NUMBERS 5.14

Assessing Statistical Significance

Name: ____ Section Number: ________

To be graded, all assignments must be completed and submitted on the original book page.

EXHIBIT 1

TABLE 5.7 Experiment Results

Group R	Time (sec)	Group L	Time (sec)
1	0.090	1	0.111
2	0.119	2	0.181
3	0.143	3	0.090
4	0.169	4	0.186
5	0.064	5	0.045
6	0.150	6	0.143

Questions

1. Find the mean of the six Group R measurements.

2. Find the mean of the six Group L measurements.

3. Calculate the difference in the means.

4. Find the standard deviation of the six Group R measurements.

5. Find the standard deviation of the six Group L measurements.

6. Follow your instructor's instructions to complete the test.

BEYOND THE NUMBERS 5.15

Hypothesis Testing—Two Means

Name: ______________________________ Section Number: ________

To be graded, all assignments must be completed and submitted on the original book page.

EXHIBIT 1

Sleep Pains

Title: Duration of Sleep Contributes to Next-day Pain Report in the General Population

Author: R. Edwards, et al.

Source: *Pain 137* (2008) 202–207.

There is a lot of interest in how disturbed sleep is related to pain perception. Throughout this study, participants from the general population recorded both the number of hours they slept and the frequency of their pain symptoms. The pain symptoms were recorded on a five-point scale: 0 = none of the time, 1 = a little, 2 = some, 3 = most, and 4 = all of the time. A summary the study results is shown in Table 5.8.

TABLE 5.8 Pain Relief Results

Sleep (Hours)	Average Pain Rating	Standard Deviation	Sample Size
0–3	1.36	1.51	75
4	1.13	1.36	166
5	0.94	1.29	434
6	0.79	1.11	1,138
7	0.73	1.11	1,568
8	0.75	1.13	1,557
9	0.71	1.09	339
10	1.24	1.4	119
11+	1.78	1.59	66

We are interested in testing:

$$H_0: \mu_1 = \mu_2$$

$$H_A: \mu_1 \neq \mu_2$$

This hypothesis concerns different pairs of sleep categories. In all cases, assume a significance level of 0.05.

Questions

1. Test the hypothesis using the patients in the 0-3 and the 5-hour sleep group.

2. Test the same hypothesis, but use the 5-hour group and the 8-hour group.

[2] There is a serious problem with testing lots of pairs of hypotheses from a single study. Doing so can complicate what one means by the Type I error rate. Your instructor may choose to elaborate.

Final Projects

American Housing Survey Data

The main objective of this project is to conduct a hypothesis test based on data from the American Housing Survey. A link to the relevant data is available at the end of this document. The two cities to be compared and the variable of interest will be assigned (Your specific cities and variable will be given in the file of project folder on Canvas). Completing the assignment using the cities and variable assigned to someone else will result in a grade of zero.

American Housing Survey Data: http://www.census.gov/programs-surveys/ahs/data/2013/ahs-2013-summary-tables/metropolitan-summary-tables---ahs-2013.html

Your submission must be a Microsoft Word document or a pdf. It will be submitted to Canvas.

Here is the paper structure:

1. **State your hypotheses.** The test will be conducted to see if there is evidence of a difference in proportions, using significance level $\alpha = 0.05$. Clearly state, in words, what the null and alternative hypotheses should be. Be as thorough as possible regarding the context – identify the two populations and the variable of interest as explicitly as you can.
2. **How was data collected for the American Housing Survey?** First, state if the American Housing Survey is an experiment or an observational study. Then, explain how the data were collected. The American Housing Survey website will display that information – you'll find it if you look around for a couple of minutes (look for the term "methodology"). Alternatively, if you Google "AHS methodology," the first link should be the one you want.
3. **Specify your two sample proportions in words and in symbols.** To find the relevant data in the Excel spreadsheet for a given city, go to the tab labeled "C-01-AH-M". The row that begins with "Sample size (number)" contains the sample data for that city. The two values you need will be in that row.
4. **Determine the *p*-value.**
   a. First, explain how the *p*-value should be computed in terms of the difference of sample proportions found in Step 3. Include an explanation of the sampling distribution. Then, using StatKey and the sample proportions found in Step 3, find the *p*-value of the hypothesis test described in Step 1. Use StatKey to generate at least 5000 randomization samples, then take a screenshot of the dot plot (with the *p*-value labeled) and the "original sample" box from StatKey and paste it in the document you submit (at the end of the document, rather than in the middle of the wording). If you want to crop the screenshot so it only includes the dot plot (and not the table on the right), use the "Print Screen" command, copy the image into MS Paint, select the part of the image containing the dot plot, copy it, and then paste it into your assignment (Don't use a phone to take a picture of a computer screen). If you are unsure how to take a screenshot, do a quick search on the internet.

   b. Use section 6.3-HT: Hypothesis test for a difference in Proportions' formula to find the standardized test statistic. Then find the *p*-value by finding the area beyond this standardized value in a standard normal distribution. Compare the two *p*-values!
5. **Make a decision about the null hypothesis, and give a formal conclusion of the test.** State whether or not your hypothesis test has a statistically significant result. Make a decision regarding the null hypothesis, and give a formal conclusion of the hypothesis test.

Statistical Inference in the Media

Portions of this project are modified from Lock, R. H. (2013). *Statistics: Unlocking the power of data* (1st ed.). Hoboken, NJ: Wiley..

This project asks you to find examples of statistical inference in the media. You are asked to find one article in the popular press where a test is described and the result is statistically significant (the article should contain the phrase "statistically significant"), and one article in the popular press where a test is described but the result is not statistically significant (the article should contain the phrase "not statistically significant"). Please do not use any of the articles from lecture notes or the workbook.

You should submit a well-written report addressing each of the following parts.

PART 1: STATISTICALLY SIGNIFICANT

Find a description of a statistical test in the popular press (such as in a magazine, newspaper, or online) and the result is statistically significant.

1. Describe how the test was conducted. How were the data collected?
2. Are the data the result of an experiment or an observational study?
3. Clearly identify (in your own well-chosen words) what the null (H_O) and alternative (H_A) appear to be in the context of this article.
4. What is a likely range for the *p*-value of this test given the information in the article (less than 5%, greater than 5%, etc.)?
5. What is the conclusion (with context) of the test?
6. Include the complete citation or web address at the end of your report.

PART 2: NOT STATISTICALLY SIGNIFICANT

Find a description of a statistical test in the popular press (such as in a magazine, newspaper, or online) but the result is not statistically significant.

1. Describe how the test was conducted. How were the data collected?
2. Are the data the result of an experiment or an observational study?
3. Clearly identify (in your own well-chosen words) what the null (H_O) and alternative (H_A) appear to be in the context of this article.
4. What is a likely range for the *p*-value of this test given the information in the article (less than 5%, greater than 5%, etc.)?
5. What is the conclusion (with context) of the test?
6. Include the complete citation or web address at the end of your report.

Conducting a Formal Survey

INTRODUCTION

The purpose of this assignment is to allow you to apply what you have learned in this course to conduct a survey, then present and interpret the results in a formal paper. You will have learned most of what you need to know to do the required tasks, but will discover some new things by doing this project. If you run into something you don't understand quite how to do, please just ask your instructor. The assignment is described below. The scope of what is required depends on whether you are being asked to do this individually or as part of a group. Your instructor will clarify for your class.

THE ASSIGNMENT

Identifying the Population: First, you are going to need to decide on a population you are interested in knowing more about (e.g., all your Facebook friends, your living community.) This needs to be a group of individuals you'll have direct access to since this is where you'll be taking your sample. The population should have at least 100 people in it.

Forming Your Questions: You need to construct questions of the following type (required):

- One question with four or fewer options. E.g. "Which of these four pop singers do you feel is most talented?" Try to ask a question that will get mixed results.
- Two related questions, each with a non-categorical (quantitative) response. E.g., "What is your current cumulative GPA?" and "Estimate how many hours you study per week."

Doing the Background Research: You need to do extensive, college-level background research into the question you are investigating in your survey. Find out what is already known about public response to those or similar questions. For example, if you ask about college food service partnering with local farmers, you should look at what other surveys similar to this one have found about public opinion on this or a similar topic. Don't just look for a count of the number of colleges that are currently partnering with local farmers. Look for the opinions that other surveys have surfaced about this question (or a related question.) Be sure not to just use anecdotal opinion as research (e.g., "Everyone I talk to in my fraternity thinks ..."). You should include at least two outside sources for this part in your paper. You should have a professional Works Cited page at the end of your paper.

Taking the Sample: Select an authentic, simple random sample (e.g., using Research Randomizer) from your population. The minimum sample size is 50 individuals. The sample MUST be a simple random sample. When selecting your population, make sure it is a group that you can use for a simple random sample.

DOING THE ANALYSIS

After you have your data, you may be required to have the following in your project. Your instructor will clarify what is required.

- A table that shows the four parameters of interest (p, μ_1, μ_2, ρ), what each parameter is in words for your survey, the estimates that you got for each from the survey, and the correct notation for each of the estimates.
- A bar chart made in Excel or Apple Numbers that exhibits the results for the question with four or fewer options.
- A 95% confidence interval for the true proportion p of individuals in the population who would have picked a particular option in the "four or fewer" options question. Use the standard error from a bootstrap distribution or the percentile method. Include a screenshot of the bootstrap distribution.
- A test of hypothesis of the form: H_0: $p = p_0$ versus H_A: $p > p_0$, $p < p_0$, or $p \neq p_0$. If possible determine a reasonable p_0 from your background research. Use a randomization distribution to complete the test and include a screenshot of the randomization distribution showing the *p*-value.
- A scatterplot produced in Excel or Apple Numbers for the two quantitative responses. Make sure the scatterplot includes the regression line and shows the equation.
- Use technology to find the correlation coefficient for the pair of quantitative responses.
- Use technology to find the slope and intercept of the regression line for the two quantitative variables. This should be shown with your scatterplot.
- A 95% confidence interval for the true average μ in the population for ONE of the quantitative variables. Use the appropriate formulas to find the interval and include a screenshot of the t^* value.
- A test of hypothesis of the form: H_0: $\mu = \mu_0$ versus H_A: $\mu = \mu_0$, $\mu < \mu_0$, or $\mu \neq \mu_0$ for the same quantitative variable you used in the confidence interval computation. If possible determine a reasonable μ_0 from your background research. Conduct the test using the appropriate formulas and include a screenshot showing your *p*-value from a *t*-distribution.

THE FINAL PAPER

Putting It All Together: Now you need to produce a professionally written report as your deliverable. Your task is to put all this work together and tell a meaningful, coherent story about the research you have done. The following is a general outline to follow when creating your paper. However, the paper should flow as a coherent piece and not simply be a bulleted list of items being checked off. Everything in the paper should be computer generated and professionally presented. The presentation of the paper, graphics, etc. will be graded.

- Develop the context for your study and explain why you decided to investigate the questions you decided to investigate and why they are important.
- Describe your population of interest and give a detailed description of how you selected your simple random sample.
- Introduce and explain your "four or fewer" options bar chart. Interpret your 95% confidence interval in terms of the parameter of interest. Clearly identify the parameter and statistic for this question in the natural flow of the paper. Clearly identify both your null and alternative hypotheses for the same variable. Test your hypothesis using a significance level of 5%. Report a *p*-value and interpret your results by giving a formal decision about H_0. Give a conclusion in context. Is the result of the hypothesis test consistent with your confidence interval? How do you know?
- Introduce your scatterplot and quantitative variables. Give and interpret your correlation coefficient for the two variables. Explain how the correlation coefficient value you calculated is consistent with your scatterplot. Give and interpret your regression slope and intercept. Does the intercept make sense?
- Interpret your 95% confidence interval for ONE of your quantitative variables in terms of the parameter of interest. Clearly identify the parameter and statistic for this question in the natural flow of the paper. Clearly identify both your null and alternative hypotheses for the same variable. Test your hypothesis using a significance level of 5%. Report a *p*-value and interpret your results by giving a formal decision about H_0. Is the result of the hypothesis test consistent with your confidence interval? How do you know?
- Reflect on your conclusions. Are they consistent with your initial research on the topic(s)? Be sure to address any non-sampling errors that may have been present and comment on anything you would do differently if you could repeat the study.
- Your work for all of your analysis should be professionally typed in an equation editor, and any relevant screenshots should be professionally included to verify your work. Make sure your work and screenshots are clearly labeled so it is clear what they are showing. These formulas and screenshots can be included in your paper, or you can put them in an appendix at the end of your paper (and reference them throughout the paper).
- The last page of your paper should include a professional Works Cited page for your research sources.

Appendix

Datasets

CANCER SURVIVAL DATA TABLE

This table is used for Beyond the Numbers 5.10 and 5.11. Please note that there are more data sets located at statconcepts.com/student-resources/sta-296-datasets.

Stomach Cancer	Bronchus Cancer	Colon Cancer	Ovarian Cancer	Breast Cancer
124	81	248	1,234	1,235
42	461	377	89	24
25	20	189	201	1,581
45	450	1,843	356	1,166
412	246	180	2,970	40
51	166	537	456	727
1,112	63	519		791
46	64	455		1,804
103	155	406		3,460
876	859	365		719
146	151	942		
340	166	776		
396	37	372		
	223	163		
	138	101		
	72	20		
	245	283		

STANDARD SCORE TABLE

Example: If a standard score, *z*, is computed to be 1.73, then one would locate 1.73 in the table (see highlighting) and corresponding *p*-value would be 0.04182 ≈ 0.04. This would then have to be compared to the preset significance level, often taken to be 0.05. This process only applies for simple hypotheses with a positive *z* score and a ">" in the alternative. Your instructor will show you how to use this table when *z* is negative and/or when the alternative is a "≠."

z	0	0.01	0.02	0.03	0.04	0.05	0.06	0.07	0.08	0.09
0	0.5	0.49601	0.49202	0.48803	0.48405	0.48006	0.47608	0.4721	0.46812	0.46414
0.1	0.46017	0.4562	0.45224	0.44828	0.44433	0.44038	0.43644	0.43251	0.42858	0.42465
0.2	0.42074	0.41683	0.41294	0.40905	0.40517	0.40129	0.39743	0.39358	0.38974	0.38591
0.3	0.38209	0.37828	0.37448	0.3707	0.36693	0.36317	0.35942	0.35569	0.35197	0.34827
0.4	0.34458	0.3409	0.33724	0.3336	0.32997	0.32636	0.32276	0.31918	0.31561	0.31207
0.5	0.30854	0.30503	0.30153	0.29806	0.2946	0.29116	0.28774	0.28434	0.28096	0.2776
0.6	0.27425	0.27093	0.26763	0.26435	0.26109	0.25785	0.25463	0.25143	0.24825	0.2451
0.7	0.24196	0.23885	0.23576	0.2327	0.22965	0.22663	0.22363	0.22065	0.2177	0.21476
0.8	0.21186	0.20897	0.20611	0.20327	0.20045	0.19766	0.19489	0.19215	0.18943	0.18673
0.9	0.18406	0.18141	0.17879	0.17619	0.17361	0.17106	0.16853	0.16602	0.16354	0.16109
1	0.15866	0.15625	0.15386	0.15151	0.14917	0.14686	0.14457	0.14231	0.14007	0.13786
1.1	0.13567	0.1335	0.13136	0.12924	0.12714	0.12507	0.12302	0.121	0.119	0.11702
1.2	0.11507	0.11314	0.11123	0.10935	0.10749	0.10565	0.10383	0.10204	0.10027	0.09853
1.3	0.0968	0.0951	0.09342	0.09176	0.09012	0.08851	0.08692	0.08534	0.08379	0.08226
1.4	0.08076	0.07927	0.0778	0.07636	0.07493	0.07353	0.07215	0.07078	0.06944	0.06811
1.5	0.06681	0.06552	0.06426	0.06301	0.06178	0.06057	0.05938	0.05821	0.05705	0.05592
1.6	0.0548	0.0537	0.05262	0.05155	0.0505	0.04947	0.04846	0.04746	0.04648	0.04551
1.7	0.04457	0.04363	0.04272	0.04182	0.04093	0.04006	0.0392	0.03836	0.03754	0.03673
1.8	0.03593	0.03515	0.03438	0.03362	0.03288	0.03216	0.03144	0.03074	0.03005	0.02938
1.9	0.02872	0.02807	0.02743	0.0268	0.02619	0.02559	0.025	0.02442	0.02385	0.0233
2	0.02275	0.02222	0.02169	0.02118	0.02068	0.02018	0.0197	0.01923	0.01876	0.01831
2.1	0.01786	0.01743	0.017	0.01659	0.01618	0.01578	0.01539	0.015	0.01463	0.01426
2.2	0.0139	0.01355	0.01321	0.01287	0.01255	0.01222	0.01191	0.0116	0.0113	0.01101
2.3	0.01072	0.01044	0.01017	0.0099	0.00964	0.00939	0.00914	0.00889	0.00866	0.00842
2.4	0.0082	0.00798	0.00776	0.00755	0.00734	0.00714	0.00695	0.00676	0.00657	0.00639
2.5	0.00621	0.00604	0.00587	0.0057	0.00554	0.00539	0.00523	0.00508	0.00494	0.0048
2.6	0.00466	0.00453	0.0044	0.00427	0.00415	0.00402	0.00391	0.00379	0.00368	0.00357
2.7	0.00347	0.00336	0.00326	0.00317	0.00307	0.00298	0.00289	0.0028	0.00272	0.00264
2.8	0.00256	0.00248	0.0024	0.00233	0.00226	0.00219	0.00212	0.00205	0.00199	0.00193
2.9	0.00187	0.00181	0.00175	0.00169	0.00164	0.00159	0.00154	0.00149	0.00144	0.00139
3	0.00135	0.00131	0.00126	0.00122	0.00118	0.00114	0.00111	0.00107	0.00104	0.001
3.1	0.00097	0.00094	0.0009	0.00087	0.00084	0.00082	0.00079	0.00076	0.00074	0.00071
3.2	0.00069	0.00066	0.00064	0.00062	0.0006	0.00058	0.00056	0.00054	0.00052	0.0005
3.3	0.00048	0.00047	0.00045	0.00043	0.00042	0.0004	0.00039	0.00038	0.00036	0.00035
3.4	0.00034	0.00032	0.00031	0.0003	0.00029	0.00028	0.00027	0.00026	0.00025	0.00024
3.5	0.00023	0.00022	0.00022	0.00021	0.0002	0.00019	0.00019	0.00018	0.00017	0.00017
3.6	0.00016	0.00015	0.00015	0.00014	0.00014	0.00013	0.00013	0.00012	0.00012	0.00011

t-TABLE

					Tail Probability *p*							
d.f.	**.25**	**.20**	**.15**	**.10**	**.05**	**.025**	**.02**	**.01**	**.005**	**.0025**	**.001**	**.005**
1	1.000	1.376	1.963	3.078	6.314	12.71	15.89	31.82	63.66	127.3	318.3	636.6
2	.816	1.061	1.386	1.886	2.920	4.303	4.849	6.965	9.925	14.09	22.33	31.60
3	.765	.978	1.250	1.638	2.353	3.182	3.482	4.541	5.841	7.453	10.21	12.92
4	.741	.941	1.190	1.533	2.132	2.776	2.999	3.747	4.604	5.598	7.173	8.610
5	.727	.920	1.156	1.476	2.015	2.571	2.757	3.365	4.032	4.773	5.893	6.869
6	.718	.906	1.134	1.440	1.943	2.447	2.612	3.143	3.707	4.317	5.208	5.959
7	.711	.896	1.119	1.415	1.895	2.365	2.517	2.998	3.499	4.029	4.785	5.408
8	.706	.889	1.108	1.397	1.860	2.306	2.449	2.896	3.355	3.833	4.501	5.041
9	.703	.883	1.100	1.383	1.833	2.262	2.398	2.821	3.250	3.690	4.297	4.781
10	.700	.879	1.093	1.372	1.812	2.228	2.359	2.764	3.169	3.581	4.144	4.587
11	.697	.876	1.088	1.363	1.796	2.201	2.328	2.718	3.106	3.497	4.025	4.437
12	.695	.873	1.083	1.356	1.782	2.179	2.303	2.681	3.055	3.428	3.930	4.318
13	.694	.870	1.079	1.350	1.771	2.160	2.282	2.650	3.012	3.372	3.852	4.221
14	.692	.868	1.076	1.345	1.761	2.145	2.264	2.624	2.977	3.326	3.787	4.140
15	.691	.866	1.074	1.341	1.753	2.131	2.249	2.602	2.947	3.286	3.733	4.073
16	.690	.865	1.071	1.337	1.746	2.120	2.235	2.583	2.921	3.252	3.686	4.015
17	.689	.863	1.069	1.333	1.740	2.110	2.224	2.567	2.898	3.222	3.646	3.965
18	.688	.862	1.067	1.330	1.734	2.101	2.214	2.552	2.878	3.197	3.611	3.922
19	.688	.861	1.066	1.328	1.729	2.093	2.205	2.539	2.861	3.174	3.579	3.883
20	.687	.860	1.064	1.325	1.725	2.086	2.197	2.528	2.845	3.153	3.552	3.850
21	.686	.859	1.063	1.323	1.721	2.080	2.189	2.518	2.831	3.135	3.527	3.819
22	.686	.858	1.061	1.321	1.717	2.074	2.183	2.508	2.819	3.119	3.505	3.792
23	.685	.858	1.060	1.319	1.714	2.069	2.177	2.500	2.807	3.104	3.485	3.768
24	.685	.857	1.059	1.318	1.711	2.064	2.172	2.492	2.797	3.091	3.467	3.745
25	.684	.856	1.058	1.316	1.708	2.060	2.167	2.485	2.787	3.078	3.450	3.725
26	.684	.856	1.058	1.315	1.706	2.056	2.162	2.479	2.779	3.067	3.435	3.707
27	.684	.855	1.057	1.314	1.703	2.052	2.158	2.473	2.771	3.057	3.421	3.690
28	.683	.855	1.056	1.313	1.701	2.048	2.154	2.467	2.763	3.047	3.408	3.674
29	.683	.854	1.055	1.311	1.699	2.045	2.150	2.462	2.756	3.038	3.396	3.659
30	.683	.854	1.055	1.310	1.697	2.042	2.147	2.457	2.750	3.030	3.385	3.646
40	.681	.851	1.050	1.303	1.684	2.021	2.123	2.423	2.704	2.971	3.307	3.551
50	.679	.849	1.047	1.299	1.676	2.009	2.109	2.403	2.678	2.937	3.261	3.496
60	.679	.848	1.045	1.296	1.671	2.000	2.099	2.390	2.660	2.915	3.232	3.460
80	.678	.846	1.043	1.292	1.664	1.990	2.088	2.374	2.639	2.887	3.195	3.416
100	.677	.845	1.042	1.290	1.660	1.984	2.081	2.364	2.626	2.871	3.174	3.390
1,000	.675	.842	1.037	1.282	1.646	1.962	2.056	2.330	2.581	2.813	3.098	3.300
∞	.674	.841	1.036	1.282	1.645	1.960	2.054	2.326	2.576	2.807	3.091	3.291
	50%	60%	70%	80%	90%	95%	96%	98%	99%	99.5%	99.8%	99.9%
					Confidence Level *C*							

Formulas

Correlation Coefficient

$$r = \frac{n(\Sigma xy) - (\Sigma x)(\Sigma y)}{\sqrt{[n\Sigma x^2 - (\Sigma x)^2][n\Sigma y^2 - (\Sigma y)^2]}}$$

Estimated Regression Line

$$\hat{y} = a + bx$$

Residual

$$\textit{observed} - \textit{predicted} = y - \hat{y}$$

95% Confidence Interval

statistic ± *margin of error*

statistic ± 2 × *standard error*

Standardized Test Statistic

$$z = \frac{\textit{statistic} - \textit{null}}{SE}$$

General Confidence Interval

statistic ± z^* × *SE*

Single Proportion Formulas

Standard Error	Confidence Interval	Test Statistic
$\sqrt{\frac{p(1-p)}{n}}$	$\hat{p} \pm z^* \sqrt{\frac{\hat{p}(1-\hat{p})}{n}}$	$z = \frac{\hat{p} - p_0}{\sqrt{\frac{p_0(1-p_0)}{n}}}$

Single Mean Formulas

Standard Error	Confidence Interval	Test Statistic
$\frac{\sigma}{\sqrt{n}}$	$\bar{x} \pm t^* \frac{s}{\sqrt{n}}$	$t = \frac{\bar{x} - \mu_0}{s/\sqrt{n}}$

Difference in Proportions Formulas

Standard Error	Confidence Interval	Test Statistic
$\sqrt{\frac{p_1(1-p_1)}{n_1} + \frac{p_2(1-p_2)}{n_2}}$	$\hat{p}_1 - \hat{p}_2 \pm z^* \sqrt{\frac{\hat{p}_1(1-\hat{p}_1)}{n_1} + \frac{\hat{p}_2(1-\hat{p}_2)}{n_2}}$	$z = \frac{\hat{p}_1 - \hat{p}_2}{\sqrt{\frac{\hat{p}(1-\hat{p})}{n_1} + \frac{\hat{p}(1-\hat{p})}{n_2}}}$

Difference in Means Formulas

Standard Error	Confidence Interval	Test Statistic
$\sqrt{\frac{\sigma_1^2}{n_1}+\frac{\sigma_2^2}{n_2}}$	$\bar{x}_1-\bar{x}_2 \pm t^*\sqrt{\frac{s_1^2}{n_1}+\frac{s_2^2}{n_2}}$	$t=\frac{\bar{x}_1-\bar{x}_2}{\sqrt{\frac{s_1^2}{n_1}+\frac{s_2^2}{n_2}}}$

Paired Difference in Means Formulas

Standard Error	Confidence Interval	Test Statistic
$\approx \frac{s_d}{\sqrt{n_d}}$	$\bar{x}_d \pm t^*\frac{s_d}{\sqrt{n_d}}$	$t=\frac{\bar{x}_d}{s_d/\sqrt{n_d}}$

Slope and Correlation

Slope Confidence Interval	Slope Test Statistic	Correlation Test Statistic
$b_1 \pm t^* \times SE$	$t=\frac{b_1}{SE}$	$t=\frac{r\sqrt{n-2}}{\sqrt{1-r^2}}$

Sample Size Calculations

Single Proportion (95%)	Single Proportion (not 95%)	Single Mean
$n=\frac{1}{ME^2}$	$n=\left(\frac{z^*}{ME}\right)\hat{p}(1-\hat{p})$	$n=\left(\frac{z^* s}{ME}\right)^2$

Degrees of Freedom

Single Mean	Difference in Means	Paired Difference in Means	Slope and Correlation
$n-1$	smaller of n_1-1 and n_2-1	n_d-1	$n-2$

z^* Table

Confidence	z*	Confidence	z*
50%	0.674	90%	1.645
60%	0.842	95%	1.960
70%	1.036	99%	2.576
80%	1.282	99.9%	3.289